CULTIVATING REGIONALISM

Cultivating Regionalism

Higher Education and the Making of the American Midwest

KENNETH H. WHEELER

NIU Press

DEKALB

© 2011 by Northern Illinois University Press

Published by the Northern Illinois University Press,
DeKalb, Illinois 60115

Library of Congress Cataloging-in-Publication Data

Wheeler, Kenneth H.
 Cultivating regionalism : higher education and the making of the American
Midwest / Kenneth H. Wheeler.
    p.   cm. — (Early American places)
 Includes bibliographical references and index.
 ISBN 978-0-87580-444-6 (cloth bound : alk. paper)
  1. Education, Higher—Middle West.   2. Universities and colleges—Middle
West.   3. Regionalism—Middle West.   I. Title.
LA230.5.M52W44   2011
378.77—dc23

                                                              2011018053

CONTENTS

ACKNOWLEDGMENTS

I gratefully thank those publishers who gave me permission to use material that appeared originally in other places. Portions of this work are drawn from "Philander Chase and College Building in Ohio," an essay in *Builders of Ohio: A Biographical History*, edited by Warren Van Tine and Michael Pierce, published by Ohio State University Press in 2003; "How Colleges Shaped a Public Culture of Usefulness," an essay in *The Center of a Great Empire: The Ohio Country in the Early American Republic*, edited by Andrew R. L. Cayton and Stuart D. Hobbs, published by Ohio University Press in 2005; and "Higher Education in the Antebellum Ohio Valley: Slavery, Sectionalism, and the Erosion of Regional Identity," published in *Ohio Valley History* 8.1 (Spring 2008): 1–22.

This work began as a dissertation completed at Ohio State University under the direction of Randolph A. Roth, who has been cheerfully supportive from the start. At Reinhardt University, my academic home, I have enjoyed the collegial goodwill both of supervisors, notably Bob Driscoll, Wayne Glowka, and the late Jerry Zeller, and of numerous colleagues, including Susan Ashmore, Theresa Ast, Donna Coffey, Anne Good, Jonathan Good, Donald Gregory, Curt Lindquist, Phil Unger, and Pam Wilson.

I am especially grateful to John Burnham, Russ Coil, Tom Hamm, Stuart Hobbs, and Randy Roth, who read the manuscript and suggested revisions, and to Jym Davis, who created the maps. Drew Cayton encouraged and improved my work at several important stages during the past two decades. Jim Madison and Amos Loveday pointed me toward the right books. Sara Hoerdeman, my editor at Northern Illinois University Press, encouraged my efforts during the review process.

The life, love, and laughter I share with my spouse, Amy Cottrill, and our daughters, Lydia and Hannah, has sustained me.

Introduction

"To be useful was the best thing the old men ever hoped for themselves, and to be aimless was their worst fear."

—MARILYNNE ROBINSON, *GILEAD*

Robert Noyce was a Midwesterner whose ideas reshaped the world. In 1927, Noyce was born in Iowa to a Congregationalist minister, Ralph, and his wife Harriet, a college graduate and former teacher, whose father and grandfather were both Congregationalist ministers as well. Robert's family life was modest and extremely pious, both in church and at home, where evenings were filled with hymns and prayers. As his mother put it, she and her husband wished "to be Christian leaders, in the best sense," to care for the poor and to treat all "people as equals, sacred in some way." Outside home and church, Robert delivered newspapers on his bicycle and shoveled snow in the winter to earn his spending money. His boyhood was also filled with mechanical pursuits. He and his brothers, fascinated by propulsion and flight, attached motors to snow sleds, lofted small hot-air balloons, built balsa-wood model airplanes, and even constructed and flew gliders from a barn roof. When he was twelve years old, Robert Noyce wrote in his journal, "My hobby is handicraft. . . . I like this hobby because it is useful."[1]

Noyce's father eventually took an administrative post within the Congregational Church, headquartered at Grinnell College, a Congregationalist school in the small town of Grinnell in central Iowa. Robert Noyce lived in the town and enrolled at the college in the 1940s. There he majored in physics, while also finding time for singing, diving, and shenanigans, one of which almost got him expelled. In 1947, his mentor, Professor of Physics Grant Gale, learned that a college friend of his from Wisconsin, John Bardeen, had invented a transistor as part of his work for Bell Laboratories in New Jersey. The creation of the transistor was a major accomplishment, one that earned Bardeen and his two co-inventors a Nobel Prize in Physics. Gale contacted Bardeen, who sent technical writings about the transistor, which Gale and Noyce studied intently during the 1947–1948 academic year. Nowhere else in the world was such academic instruction occurring, except at this small college in a small town in Iowa. When Noyce showed up at the Massachusetts Institute of Technology for graduate work, his professors, if they had even heard of transistors, had not studied them.[2]

Little interested in theoretical research, Noyce gravitated toward experiment. Ph.D. in hand, he worked first at Philco before he went to California, where he became a founder of Fairchild Semiconductor and an inventor of the integrated circuit, often called a silicon chip, or microchip. Thinking back to an era in the 1950s when a single computer filled a large room, it is difficult to overemphasize how revolutionary Noyce's invention was. People throughout the world today utilize microchips constantly—they are the basis of the home computer, the Internet, cell phones, microwave ovens, global positioning systems, compact disk players, satellites, and cable television.[3]

Robert Noyce also created more than just the microchip—he inaugurated a business culture with worldwide ramifications in what became known as Silicon Valley. At a time when the East Coast model of hierarchical business structures replete with symbols of corporate power reigned, Noyce set up operations in a nondescript warehouse. Hierarchies were purposely flattened. Nobody had corner offices on top floors. Workers did not even have cubicles, but desks with low partitions so they could interact with each other. Instead of eating power lunches, they ordered submarine sandwiches delivered to everybody. Instead of being chauffeured in fancy limos, the scientists drove themselves and parked in the common parking lot. Seniority and rank did not matter—ideas did. And ideas were worth money. Noyce, years later, was a founder of Intel Corporation, which would dominate the microchip industry, and he was a millionaire many, many times over.[4]

Noyce's life contained seeming contradictions. He was a millionaire capitalist who created an egalitarian workplace. He was a pathbreaking scientist who came from a devout family and a denominational college. He was a small-town Midwesterner who profoundly influenced the culture of Silicon Valley, one of the most significant centers of research and development in the world during the late twentieth century.

Yet this is not a book about Robert Noyce. Rather, this book is about the cultural region that shaped him. Noyce inherited and was formed within a regional culture that emphasized productivity and usefulness, had a rich history of egalitarianism in social institutions, and valued creativity and new ideas. Today, we are unaccustomed to thinking of the Midwest, especially its small towns and religiously affiliated colleges, as a source of science and invention, as trendsetting and innovative. The temptation is to think of Noyce as an anomaly. But Noyce's values and his habits make sense when we understand the regional culture in which he matured.

Telling Robert Noyce's story is an appropriate and helpful way to establish the themes of this book. Though I focus on the antebellum West a century before Noyce's early life, his cultural roots bring into relief central aspects of the region that have not been adequately explored by scholars, resulting in some misconceptions about central characteristics of the region. The cultural characteristics of the antebellum West I examine in this book were exemplified and sustained most noticeably by the region's many small denominational colleges. Grinnell, Noyce's alma mater, was such a college. In the context of this study, Noyce's experience at Grinnell meant more than simply preparation for the moment he made it to MIT. Rather, Grinnell was just one of a great number of Western colleges founded during the antebellum period that both reflected and shaped a developing Western culture, and had much to do with the perspective and values of Robert Noyce.[5]

Founding Western Colleges

In colonial America people founded a small number of colleges, and a few more emerged in the decades following the American Revolution. But during the antebellum decades, from 1820 onward, Americans founded hundreds of colleges, and in no region did more colleges appear than in the West. There, for both structural and cultural reasons, Westerners built their colleges differently from New Englanders and Southerners and charted a new path in American higher education.[6]

The population of the West was extraordinarily diverse, and these people created communities in places regulated, in part, by the federal Land Ordinance of 1785 and the Northwest Ordinance of 1787. The resulting relatively dense development, with so many towns and so many religious denominations, underlay the conditions that led to so many colleges being founded. Because Western state governments made acquisition of a college charter easy, Western college founders represented a wider variety of denominations than founders in other regions. Townspeople eagerly supported colleges because they knew that colleges brought both improved chances of economic prosperity and an improved quality of civic and religious life. Almost always, religious denominations partnered with towns in support of a college. The result was a proliferation of denominational colleges throughout the region.

As they founded their numerous colleges, these founders departed from the paths of development in Eastern and Southern states. Westerners supported manual labor programs, which helped nonelite students pay for their collegiate education. This pattern differed from Eastern and Southern colleges, which eliminated manual labor in favor of gymnastics in the East and military drill in the South. The manual labor programs of Westerners reflected an interest in productive labor, and an egalitarian streak among Westerners who did not want their college graduates to be far removed from the experiences of common farmers and tradespeople.

A largely Protestant emphasis on usefulness, both to God and to society, paved the way for collegiate coeducation. Many Westerners, from a more rural background and with a lower class status, did not face the same obstacles to coeducation as in other regions, where more elite college founders and leaders desired more rigidly separate gender roles, and where the idea of collegiate coeducation brought with it suspicions of less rigorous education and a whiff of impropriety. Western religious denominations that were the most likely to let women preach were the groups most likely to admit women into their colleges. This combination of pragmatic Protestant evangelicalism and views rooted in the life experience of nonelite rural Westerners, mixed with the ease with which denominations could secure collegiate charters, paved the way to widespread collegiate coeducation in the West, a phenomenon virtually unknown in the antebellum East and South.

On campus, a climate of religiosity and respect for professorial authority contributed to a civil culture of purposeful debate. The students of the Western colleges, compared to their counterparts in the East and South, behaved differently because of their nonelite status. One chief measure of this difference is that Western college students never rioted during the antebellum period. The ethos of the colleges fostered peaceful means of resolving conflicts. As students by the thousands left these colleges to teach schools or make their way in the world, they carried many of the values of the colleges with them.

The final chapter of this book offers two answers, though perhaps many more exist, to the question of what the implications of these Western colleges were over time. First, this regional culture of the Midwest reached an apex during the Progressive era, from about 1890 to 1920, a profoundly important period of American reform and creativity. The leaders of the Progressives came disproportionately from the Midwest, many of them graduates of the denominational colleges. These were the years when the term "Middle West" became associated with the region because Americans recognized that something was happening in that region and they needed a recognizable name for it. This was the place where Jane Addams started Hull House, where Wilbur and Orville Wright invented the airplane, where Frank Lloyd Wright launched new architectural styles. This was where William Rainey Harper built the University of Chicago, where Thorstein Veblen criticized conspicuous consumption, where Eugene Debs poked at Americans' social conscience. This was the region where John Dewey's ideas challenged existing educational theories, where Henry Ford revolutionized automobility, where Theodore Dreiser penned great literature. This was the Midwest of Frederick Jackson Turner's frontier thesis, Harvey W. Wiley's Food and Drug Act, and leadership from politicians such as Robert M. La Follette, working with University of Wisconsin Progressives to use educational resources for social betterment. During these decades, the Midwest was dynamic.[7]

Second, one of the values that Progressives held dear was a belief in science. Unsurprisingly, the Midwestern colleges proved remarkably propitious to science as a means of intellectual inquiry and a career. Nationally, during the late nineteenth and early twentieth centuries, colleges clustered in the Midwest produced the highest percentages of graduates who became scientists.[8] Robert Noyce was notable, but he was following long-standing traditions and regional patterns. The prominence of scientific inquiry in the Midwestern colleges connects to the class and cultural values of the antebellum Western colleges. The educational world in which productive, manual labor was valued, egalitarian coeducation was emphasized, and the regional culture was open to new ideas, led naturally to a career choice of science, with its antibourgeois status, its emphasis on experimentation and receptivity to new possibilities, and its propensity toward usefulness. My explanation is not designed to praise or justify the antebellum colleges, but rather to open up ways of seeing what these colleges meant, and continued to mean, within the regional culture of which they were so much a part.

Method

In this study I use the antebellum Western colleges as a prism through which to explore the ways Westerners imagined themselves and acted upon their thoughts. In these colleges people were translating the values of an imagined community—their identity as Westerners—into an institution, the college. The colleges helped to amplify these values, and served as a crucial institution within the formation of a regional identity.[9]

This Western identity formed over time, and did not exist in a full-fledged fashion in the 1820s and 1830s. Yet regional identification, an imagined community, shaped tangibly what the West became through public policy, private and collective efforts, individual decisions, and cultural expressions of values. Westerners talked about who they believed they were and what traits inhered in the place they called home. Sometimes people invoked their Western identity when they changed the kind of colleges they built, who could run them, who came to college, the curriculum offered, the climate on campus, and consequently the meaning of the education provided.

Of course, there is more than one story to tell about the origins of the Midwest, more than one lens through which to envisage the identity of this region. No culture is monolithic, and neither was the culture of the antebellum West and eventually the Midwest. One can find within that regional culture various facets and subcultures, some of which are diffuse or even contradictory. This work is not, for example, a study of elites, politics, or urban culture, and is limited to a focus on collegiate education and the insights that can come from such a focus.

Yet what happened in higher education heralded larger changes in the culture of the region—in thought and action, creation, invention, and experimentation—with implications that continue in the present. Indeed, the primary sources show that the small colleges were central to the formation of the whole regional culture. Not only were there dozens of colleges, but many people across the region were tied to them through religious denominations, students or graduates they knew, or proximity. Though only a small percentage of people attended the colleges, these students had a disproportionate influence in the region as they fanned out and taught schools, preached to congregants, and participated in civic life.

In order to understand what happened in the West, I have used a wide range of source materials to uncover the experiences and ideas of people associated with the colleges. College founders expressed ideas about the schools they sought to create. The correspondence of professors and supporters, among others, tells how these schools operated and how people experienced their education. Students wrote in diaries and penned letters to parents and friends. Literary societies kept minutes. Colleges produced catalogs that explained the purpose of the school, the curriculum, and the rules. Speakers delivered lectures that were subsequently published. Educational, denominational, and local presses published news about education. As I studied these materials and compared them to what we know about higher education elsewhere in the nation, I discerned several patterns. I have come to several conclusions about the developing ideas and values of the West and Midwest.

Findings and Implications

In the antebellum West, a heterogeneous array of religious denominations, in combination with town sponsors and state legislatures liberal with collegiate charters, resulted in numerous colleges in a diverse and loosely controlled landscape of higher education.

Nonelite students gained access to these Western colleges, especially through manual labor programs, which broke from the norms of classical education.

Manual labor programs were especially popular among Western college supporters, often farmers, who had an egalitarian and producer-culture mentality.

This same mentality, coupled with a desire that people be useful, led Westerners to introduce collegiate coeducation.

Because of this distinctive student body and a campus climate that encouraged religiosity, debate, and civility, Western college students sought changes through reasoned, peaceful means and did not riot during the antebellum period.

The regional culture of the Midwest reached an apex of influence and generativity during the Progressive era.

As support for manual labor evolved into support for scientific agriculture and general scientific inquiry, the Midwestern colleges were highly productive of graduates who became scientists in the late nineteenth and early twentieth centuries.

* * *

These findings advance historical understanding of the development of higher education in the antebellum West, and suggest a trajectory and meaning of the Midwest as a cultural region that is largely absent from existing scholarship.

In chapter 1, I explain the basis of antebellum Western higher education. In the West, a wide variety of religious denominations desired colleges, a large number of towns eagerly hosted these colleges, and, of critical importance, state legislatures freely chartered denominationally controlled colleges and rarely set limits on the colleges they established. As a result, Westerners founded more colleges than people elsewhere. This diverse and loosely controlled environment for higher education opened greater possibilities for creative innovation than existed in other regions. Chapter 2 details why producer-minded Westerners preferred manual labor programs over gymnastics and military drill. A related egalitarian mindset that valued usefulness, and the lack of rigid separation of the sexes, accounts for why Westerners endorsed coeducation, the subject of chapter 3. In the fourth chapter, I demonstrate that the students of the Western colleges behaved differently from students in other regions because of their nonelite status, their penchant for debate, and a religious campus climate that fostered peaceful methods of resolving conflicts. The final chapter follows students from these Western colleges into the late nineteenth century and the Progressive era, describes that period from a Midwestern perspective, and illuminates one aspect of the unfolding of Midwestern culture and history during the twentieth century through a discussion of scientists and the world of Robert Noyce.

1 / Building Western Colleges

In 1860, a young man in Massachusetts had his choice of four, perhaps five, colleges in the state. A young woman in Massachusetts had no schools recognized as colleges available to her. In Ohio the same man could enter one of two dozen different colleges, and a woman could enroll at a half dozen of those same colleges. These comparisons could be made between Connecticut and Indiana, or South Carolina and Illinois. Many colleges operated in the West, and not nearly so many existed in the states along the Atlantic.[1]

The differences that account for the widely varied number of colleges in these disparate places were both structural and cultural. Federal policies embedded within the Land Ordinance of 1785 and the Northwest Ordinance of 1787 laid the groundwork for an incredibly diverse population that ranged over these lands and built the towns that would host the colleges. Scores of religious denominations worked actively to shape the society that was emerging in the West, in part by founding colleges. State legislatures facilitated this process by issuing collegiate charters freely. The mixture of these forces resulted in a landscape of higher education different from that in other areas of the United States and other countries.

In the decades following the American Revolution, white settlers poured into the lands of the West from all parts of the existing United States, removing and displacing existing American Indian peoples as they came. The settlers who came into the region often made their homes in new communities composed primarily of others from the same origins.

Ohio's Virginia Military District, for example, was settled primarily by Virginians and Kentuckians, while the Western Reserve along Lake Erie was the endpoint for many a New England traveler. Many other areas, large and small, had their distinctive stamps. Quakers, many of them Southerners, moved to Indiana's White Water Valley, and of course the myriad Pennsylvanians—German, English, Scotch-Irish—filled in everywhere. It was indeed, as Andrew Cayton has pointed out, the most diverse place in the world at that time.[2]

With this incredible array of people came a remarkable diversity in religion. The West was settled during the time that Nathan Hatch saw "The Democratization of American Christianity," a period after the American Revolution when state-supported churches withered and a burst of religiosity, particularly within groups that did not rely on political support, transformed religion in the United States as a host of small and large denominations competed with one another for adherents in an unregulated environment. G. M. Beswick, a Methodist from Centreville, Indiana, wrote to Asbury Wilkinson in 1846 and reported: "We have many isms to contend with in this section of the state. Among the exclusionists we have the Romanist, the Puseyite, the Seceder, the Quaker, the hardshell Baptist (very few), and the Campbellite." As if that were not enough to compete against, Beswick noted, "among the other isms we have a kind of supernatural Deism, the skum of every other ism. Here too are the Scootites, and the 'United Brethren' . . . And we have a few dough faced Coumberlands here." A similar situation prevailed in most parts of the region. Groups such as the Methodists and the Baptists gathered in millions of members, while a vast number of other denominations operated in their own ways in a variety of places.[3]

Structurally, when they arrived, they were moving into a part of the country overseen by the federal government through, in part, the Land Ordinance of 1785. The Land Ordinance of 1785 mattered because it created a township-based rectangular system of surveying, as opposed to a method of indiscriminate location, and thus fostered a much more intensive pattern of settlement and of road-building, with relatively small farms. Over time, portions of this Northwest Territory filled enough that they became states. Ohio was first in 1803, followed by Indiana (1816), Illinois (1818), Michigan (1835), and Wisconsin (1848).[4]

The groups of Western settlers in these places, with their multiplicity of distinctive origins and cultural ways, initially settled in a kind of mosaic or patchwork quilt across the landscape. But there was, from the first, a large amount of interaction because of the geography of the land. The Ohio River was a natural highway along the southern edge of this region that transported people, goods, and ideas. And the Great Lakes provided another natural passageway along the northern portion of the West. In between, there were no mountain ranges to interfere with travel. Instead, a number of navigable rivers, old paths trod by American Indians, and eventually canals, roads (including the National Road), and railroads integrated the region. People mingled constantly. In 1829, John Durkee wrote from Lafayette, Indiana, "our country is settled with Emigrants from almost every state in the Union." Similarly, in 1832, Mary Hovey, living in Fountain County in central Indiana, wrote to her sister that "our society here is made of people from so many different states & countries it is almost impossible to speak of any general character."[5]

Additionally, the structure of the Northwest Territory encouraged collegiate education, in part because of the prohibition against slavery during the territorial period. Usually when people think about education and the Northwest Ordinance of 1787, they point to the section that reads "schools and the means of education shall always be encouraged." But the Northwest Ordinance also affected education indirectly, through its ban on slavery during the territorial period. Partly as a consequence, no state that emerged from the Northwest Territory legalized slavery. This situation, in combination with high wages and low land prices, helped to prevent the plantations that absorbed so many town functions in the American South. Theodore Benson has postulated that the presence and lack of slavery in Mississippi and Indiana, respectively, formed the foundation of their disparate antebellum development. Sectional differences, argued Benson, were not so much the result of ideological constructions, such as planter hegemony or marked differences in racial attitudes among whites. Rather, the consequences of slavery and the lack of slavery were the most important determinants of the course of development in Mississippi and Indiana. In Mississippi, because of the legality of slavery, large plantations dominated the landscape and stunted the growth of towns and commercial development, which depended upon a populous hinterland. Consequently, voluntary organizations were fewer, religious denominations less diverse, and political constituencies not as varied as in Indiana. In Indiana, the prohibition of slavery led to numerous small family farms and higher population densities that encouraged the growth of small towns. The result of this societal structure was a broad economic, religious, and social diversity that generated a vigorous "intellectual economy" in which antebellum Hoosiers were open to new ideas and to cultural innovation.[6]

That intellectual economy depended heavily on towns. Small towns were everywhere in the antebellum West, a region with at least five times as many towns per capita as the Deep South. Westerners founded their towns for many reasons. Some towns were governmental centers, with land offices, state capitals, or county courthouses. Other towns grew at important transportation junctures, particularly on navigable waterways. Some towns existed to house workers who extracted nearby natural resources, or who worked in manufacturing. Other towns served religious, educational, or health concerns. Most towns functioned as markets for area farmers.[7]

These towns competed with each other for economic survival and improvement, and one way for a town to do well was to have a college. When Philander Chase was looking for a place to found his college in Ohio in the middle 1820s, he was inundated with requests from townspeople who wished to host his college. Thus, when Chase considered purchasing land in Knox County in central Ohio, he reported to his wife that two *"selfish"* men he spoke to were "dead set against the Knox County plan as such because it would (in their opinion) divert the travelling from Berkshire to Sunbury and there be no gain but rather an injury to their property!!!" Chase wearily complained that "the local interests of several little towns, and villages amongst us so far warp the judgment of many that I apprehend great difficulty" in establishing the college. Chase "feared" that "such is the overbearing influence of local interests that" all the advantages that would come from having the college in the countryside "will be overlooked and disregarded for the sole purpose of building up the importance of little towns and villages."[8]

At that time, many Westerners embraced ideas of unlimited progress, represented, for example, in the perfectionistic impulses of evangelical religion so prevalent during the Second Great Awakening. Landowners' desires for higher land values were intertwined with goals of civic and moral improvement. Timothy Smith, in his study of antebellum colleges in Indiana and Illinois, found that almost every college had connections to land speculation. Educators saw their involvement with raising the prices of land and trying to buy cheap and sell dear as perfectly compatible with their Christian beliefs. This easy combination of practicality and idealism was a hallmark of the culture of the region.[9]

One example of this behavior is provided by John J. Shipherd. Born in 1802 in West Greenville, New York, Shipherd became a minister in Elyria, Ohio, before he became a college founder. He helped raise the money to buy 5,000 acres of land that became Oberlin, both a religious colony and a college. Three years later in 1836 he wrote to his parents, "my *usefulness* requires that I should leave Oberlin. . . . All that Oberlin can educate on the manual labor plan will not be a hundreth part of the youth that now wait for Oberlin privileges." Shipherd therefore planned to "establish several Oberlins" and "form a Western Education company for the establishment of Ob.n 2d—Obn 3d &c." For financing, Shipherd had raised pledges of funds and was then "to select & purchase the most eligible site for a manual labour institution. The design is to get 10,000 acres & to raise money enough on the sale of it to endow the college, & aid O[berlin]. some $10,000. In addition to this enough to make a second purchase for a Theological Sem, from which enough must be saved for a *third purchase*, & so on."[10]

In effect, Shipherd was planning a franchising program in which the money raised from buying land and founding a college on the property, then selling the rest of the land at a profit (because of the college effect on raising property values), would finance the next land purchase and college, etc. Shipherd's plans did not proceed as he had anticipated, but he went on to found both the LaGrange Collegiate Institute in Indiana and Olivet College in Michigan.[11]

Wherever founders went, they wound up working with towns, not cities. In the antebellum West, the largest city, Cincinnati, with 25,000 residents in 1830 and 115,000 by 1850, did not support colleges as stable or as large as numerous other Western towns with populations of fewer than 2,000. This same pattern obtained elsewhere in the West. In 1850 in Michigan, the only city with more than 3,000 residents, Detroit, did not support a college. In Indiana, the three largest cities in 1850, each with a population of 8,000, did not have a college until Indianapolis hosted one not far from the city in the 1850s. Wisconsin had no urban centers; the largest city in Illinois, Chicago, had no colleges until the very end of the antebellum period.[12]

Contemporaries claimed that towns made better locations than cities for education. The 1848 catalogue of Franklin College, of New Athens, Ohio, for instance, explained that the location of the village of New Athens in relation to the Steubenville turnpike, the National Road, and the Ohio River was "sufficiently near these thoroughfares and large places to enjoy their advantages, sufficiently remote to be free from their vices." Franklin "promote[d] the successful prosecution of study, and the culture and preservation of morals, being secluded from all those allurements from study, haunts of dissipation and abandoned associates so prejudicial to youth in large places." Similarly, the 1852 catalogue of Michigan

Central College described Spring Arbor as "a pleasant country town, free from the temptations and distracting influences incidental to a large village, and unsurpassed in healthiness."[13] Notice of the wholesomeness of the college and town was ubiquitous in annual college catalogues of the period. Whatever the reasoning and the forces that created this situation, the effect was to remove Western higher education from centers of political power and wealth. The Western college experience was rustic.

This was a time in American history when religious denominations were the driving force behind the expansion of education. Townspeople did not found colleges alone; if they could have, Philander Chase would not have been pursued by so many people who wanted him to place his college in their town. In almost all cases, colleges relied upon denominational connections for survival. Even if denominations did not ordinarily aid colleges directly, members of denominations and sometimes denominational aid societies often supported denominational colleges. Colleges depended upon supportive denominations not only for dollars, but for leadership—able teachers, administrators, fund-raisers, and lobbyists. And most denominational members desired colleges that would provide seminary training to members who would then serve the church. Denominational preachers encouraged members of their congregations to send their children to a college associated with the denomination.[14]

A prime example of this relationship between towns and denominations comes from Delaware, Ohio, where Methodists created Ohio Wesleyan University. In the 1830s in Delaware, the main attraction was a resort hotel. This was a time when Americans sometimes went to spas or springs for their health, and the resort hotel catered to tourists and convalescents who came to enjoy a sulphurous spring of healing waters on the south side of Delaware. But in 1841 the resort hotel went out of business. Perhaps the sulphurous smell drove away the customers. As one observer noted, "Almost the first sense greeted upon arrival" in Delaware "was that of smell. What peculiar odor, as of spoiled eggs half-cooked, invades the nostrils? A friend explains that it is the 'Sulphur Spring.' It was not at all delightful, certainly."[15]

The closing of the hotel mattered also because no one was likely to come to Delaware otherwise, given the condition of the roads. One person reported that in the early 1840s "the town was almost inaccessible except during the summer and early autumn months." A stage line passed through Delaware traveling between Columbus and Sandusky, but when "the mud was deep the wheels often sank in the road-bed up to the hubs. The ruts too . . . were uneven, the wagons tilting up on one side or the other alternately . . . . They were in constant danger of overturning." One clever Buckeye composed a bit of doggerel on the subject.

> The road was impassible—
> Not even jackassable;
> And all those who travel it
> Should turn out and gravel it.

Moreover, the town of Delaware was an unimpressive village of 900, with a few sidewalks, but no paved streets.[16]

In this situation, with their boarded-up hotel beside a stinky spring of water, the people of Delaware proved resourceful. Late in 1841 Delaware residents approached the Methodist church in Ohio about founding a college, with the hotel to become the academic building. The people of Delaware would donate the building, along with ten acres it stood upon, if the Methodists would found a college there. At the time, Ohio Methodists were looking for a place to found a college in a central place in the state. Since the 1820s they had partnered with Kentucky Methodists in support of Augusta College along the Ohio River in Kentucky, but that arrangement had become unsatisfactory. The Methodists were intrigued; they sent a delegation to Delaware to inspect the place. The delegation made a favorable recommendation, so the Methodists applied to the state legislature for a college charter, which the state legislature granted on March 7, 1842. The Methodists were not prepared to start their college the very next day, but they put together a preparatory school immediately, and the actual college (which still consisted mostly of boys doing preparatory work) began in 1844, led by two faculty members and an assistant teacher. With the support of a board of trustees and a few Methodists who traveled the state in search of students and funds, Ohio Wesleyan was up and running.[17]

When the first president, Edward Thomson, arrived in 1846, he devoted his inaugural address at commencement to an explanation of how Delaware was improved with a college. Thomson reflected on the circumstances whereby the college came to be located in Delaware, and then he examined the *"prospects"* of the institution, which he said were "founded upon *the interests of the citizens of Delaware.* The institution originated with them, and their personal pride is involved in its success." Thomson reminded his listeners that the "University promotes the *wealth* of the town." He then detailed the financial implications, from faculty salaries to student expenditures, to new residents who had moved to Delaware because of the college, as well as travelers who spent money when they came to visit students or professors. All told, Thomson reckoned, not counting the new businesses that were opening up, or the 20 percent increase in property values, Ohio Wesleyan annually contributed $15,750 to the economic life of the town.[18]

These economic benefits, though, were rivaled by the "indirect" advantages. A town such as Delaware, lacking the opportunities of a port city, for example, would have to rely upon the intelligence of its inhabitants for prosperity. Parents could send their children to school, yet these schools needed "competent teachers, without which the school is a farce and a curse. Where are you to obtain these?" asked Thomson. "At the college." Graduates could direct schools and examine potential teachers, while college professors would write the needed textbooks.[19]

A college also awakened interest in education within the entire community. Thomson imagined for his listeners that a "farmer, coming to the seat of learning to dispose of his produce, hears a favorable account of the students, and finding that he can support his son at the University . . . determines to send him one session." The farmer's son does well, the parents are pleased and proud, and his siblings also are drawn to "the flowery paths of knowledge." "He now organizes a debating club, and is elected president; he establishes a library, and is made librarian; he delivers a lecture on astronomy, and excites general admiration." The neighbors notice and the family rises in their esteem. "Well, father, exclaim the youths, in a dozen cabins at once, we will go to college, too." Thomson theorized that "this circle of emulation is constantly widening," resulting in "a gradual elevation of the whole platform of society. Industry is stimulated, intelligence diffused, improvements introduced, the public taste refined, enterprise provoked, acquaintance extended, and correspondence with distant points established." These graduates would fill important positions in civic life, and their education would also erode the distinctions created by differences in wealth, and create a more harmonious, unified society.[20]

Thomson's rhetoric was grandiose, and yet the evidence shows he was right in many ways, and there were other influences he did not mention and could not foresee, patterns of interaction and connection that emerged over the years that strongly influenced Delaware, the county, and the college. For one, Thomson himself delivered every Sunday afternoon a "lecture-sermon." Faculty and students attended, but the audience was also composed of the lawyers, the doctors, the clergy, and others who were most educated. One pupil remarked that the "students by scores were often crowded out of their seats by strangers staying in town over Sabbath to hear Dr. Thomson."[21] Here were "acquaintances extended" and "the public taste refined."

Faculty members did far more than teach their charges; they were involved in community life. Frederick Merrick, one of the early faculty members, was particularly active. As a later president reported, when Merrick first moved to town, immediately he began "at the Court House a union prayer-meeting for the promotion of sympathy and fellowship between the churches. He called on every minister, and attended every church in the town." Merrick also crusaded against alcohol, but, as the president related, "while he was an uncompromising foe of the saloons . . . no man was a more tender friend to the saloon-keeper. He made an annual visit to each one of these men, treating each as a fellow-citizen, and talking with him about his plans for time, and for eternity." Merrick also visited the poor more often than anyone else in town.[22]

As part of these calls upon the poor, Merrick tried to build Methodism in Delaware. For example, at the beginning of the 1850s, many workers on the new railroad being built east of the Olentangy River lived on that side of the river and had no church. Merrick, on a summer Sunday afternoon, crossed the river and stood on the railroad depot platform and sang a hymn, which attracted a few listeners. He then prayed and preached a short sermon. These small beginnings in East Delaware led, eventually, to church buildings and Sunday schools (which, in that time, offered instruction later taken up by public schools). Likewise, Merrick did the same thing in southwestern Delaware, where his Sunday school became the basis for the erection of a chapel.[23]

Students also involved themselves in civic life. In the 1840s, as faculty member William G. Williams described it, the "University grounds, while not a public common, were often the common pasture of the town, overrun by cows and hogs; the surface was mostly as nature left it, rough, ungraded, brushy, and in the low ground, swampy." Rather than tromp through the mud, "every winter the students clubbed together and had spent tanbark hauled from the tanneries and spread all the way from the college doors as far up as to William Street. . . . This was a temporary expedient, of course, but it served to keep the feet out of the mire during the season." These students needed to go into town, as the college did not house many, and did not feed any. Students routinely roomed or boarded, or both, with town families, which augmented the income of area residents. Ohio Wesleyan argued that the practice kept "the students under family influences and brings the citizens into kind relations with the institution." Also, every Ohio Wesleyan catalogue contained a statement that explained, "On Sabbath morning all the students are required to attend public worship in town, at such Church as the Faculty understand to be preferred by the parents or guardian. In the afternoon, they attend at the College Chapel, for the usual religious exercises, with a sermon or a lecture on some portion of the Scripture." The students who were exempt were those "licensed to preach," who often spent their Sundays in the pulpit of some little church miles from Delaware.[24]

Thomson was right that people wanted to move to a town with a college. Delaware grew from 900 townspeople in 1840 to 4,000 by 1860. And the people who came generally valued education. In a letter to Ohio Wesleyan, a Kentuckian wrote, "The Lord has given us six children to train and educate. [A]nd we beleive it to be our duty to given them a good education—this we cannot do in Kentucky for the very simple reason that our income will not warrant the great outlay that is required here to educate. But in Ohio where the withering blight of slavery is not felt, even the poor mans child may be fitted for a life of usefulness and honor." The writer went on to ask about the prospects for purchasing land in Delaware and finding employment as a blacksmith.[25]

The growth of the college spurred additional educational developments in Delaware. In 1853, for example, Delaware hosted a Teacher's Institute at which notable Ohio educators gave lectures. This event would likely not have occurred in Delaware without the existence of the college. And though Ohio Wesleyan failed to join the vanguard of coeducational colleges, Delaware residents began the Ohio Wesleyan Female College in 1853. The Female College president explained that "[t]he rapid progress in the growth of the O. W. University, and consequent influx of a population, often of entire families, for educational purposes, and the desire of others from abroad to have their sons and daughters associated as nearly as may be, in their educational efforts, made it very desirable that, with an institution for young men, there should be one for young women." Discussion of coeducation began immediately, and the two schools merged in 1877.[26]

As Ohio Wesleyan University and the Ohio Wesleyan Female College flourished, Delaware grew and became more important. Townspeople built better roads, a sewer system, and a water drainage system. Most important, the college students were the decisive factor in making Delaware a stop on the Cleveland & Columbus Railroad. The railroad builders initially planned to take their railroad directly through Delaware County to the east of the county seat. They built the railroad that way in the early 1850s, later adding a curve that took in the city of Delaware, even though most of the railroad traffic ran the straight route and bypassed the town. But eventually the railroad company executives realized that with "four or five hundred students making several trips over the road each year," it was most advantageous to make the curve the standard route. Without the college students, the railroad would have bypassed Delaware permanently. With those students, the new railroad route integrated Delaware into a growing transportation network within the state and nation.[27]

Delaware reaped the benefits of the railroad immediately, as the first passenger train to come along the curve carried the famous Hungarian Louis Kossuth, who was touring the United States and stopped in Delaware in February 1852. More speakers followed. The annual college commencement, which townspeople routinely attended, brought speakers, including William Holmes McGuffey. During the 1850s Delaware was a regular stop on a lecture circuit that brought literary figures, among others, to towns across the West. Having a railroad pass through, and a college that provided a forum, attracted speakers, who raised the level of sophistication and connected Delaware to a wider world of politics, religion, and literature.[28]

The colleges in Delaware also served as "nerve centers" of the town's organizational life. In the 1850s, the Delaware Library Association and the Delaware Young Men's Lecture Association were certainly supported by persons connected to the colleges. Other organizations existed entirely within these educational institutions. In 1846, for example, Ohio Wesleyan University students founded the Allen Missionary Lyceum "to increase our interest, & improve our knowledge in the subject of christian missions." For decades, members held prayer meetings for mission work, attracted speakers, and hosted discussions on issues faced by missions and missionaries.[29]

Along with voluntary associations, the college provided leaders in civic life. At the dedication of Oak Grove cemetery in 1851, the "exercises" included prayer by President Thomson and a "dedicatory address" from Professor Merrick. William G. Williams not only taught at the college, but also served for 21 years on the Delaware City School Board, and worked about as long on the Board of County School Examiners. Graduates also served. John Doddridge Van Deman, class of 1854, was mayor of Delaware for three terms. Another graduate, class of 1857, William Semans, returned to the University as a professor, served as mayor of Delaware in the middle 1870s, and was a school examiner for Delaware County for a dozen years.[30]

Edward Thomson would not have been surprised at all of these events. He predicted them. What he was most right about, though, was that the founding of Ohio Wesleyan University was the pivotal moment in the history of the town—because the college was a statement of values. Had the hotel not failed, Delaware might have remained a resort town. It would have grown and developed in very different ways. The presence of the college, with its president, faculty, and students, had everything to do with the kind of place, and the kind of people who inhabited that place, that Delaware became.

More generally, in the Western states founders often justified colleges because colleges produced excellent and Christian citizens. While the motive of producing citizenship was not strong at the beginning of college-founding, people soon concluded that the church ought to cultivate "civic leadership," and they saw the denominational college as an ideal vehicle through which to accomplish that end. Christians knew that their developing society in the West would require leading citizens and, increasingly, they sought to make sure that those citizens received their education at a Christian college. Better to be led as a society by Christian doctors, lawyers, and teachers than not, and to have these educated laypersons sit in the pews of the churches.[31]

Some people argued for more colleges in the West because poorer students would be able to avail themselves of an education, and the United States would be stronger thereby. Philander Chase, the Episcopal founder of Kenyon College, made this argument in 1827 while he addressed the Ohio state legislature as he sought support for his bid to the United States Congress for a grant of government lands for the support of Kenyon. Chase justified his request on the basis of Kenyon's centrality in the education of schoolteachers. He told the legislators that the Western population lacked sufficient schoolteachers and remained poorly educated. He argued that Ohio should have more schoolteachers and that Ohioans should "educate these Teachers ourselves. Let us draw from our own soil the moral seed, by which the Western country is to be supplied with the fruits of learning." Western colleges needed adequate support "so that the expense of education will come within the reach of all." The colleges should train schoolteachers, Chase believed, "from the middle and more industrious walks of life; the sons of farmers and mechanics in our country, who have witnessed the necessity, who have felt the want, and, to the welfare of our Republic, who know the great importance of *common learning*."[32]

In addition, Chase maintained, Kenyon provided a civic function by upholding the civil structure of the United States. The teachers who went forth from Kenyon College would be "the surest preservative of our constitutional liberties." Chase argued that the Constitution prohibited "privileged orders of men," and that a college education must, thus, be accessible to all. "But experience does not justify this reasonable expectation," warned Chase. "Such is the foundation of our Colleges, especially those in the Atlantic States, that NO POOR MAN, nor even one in moderate circumstances, can give his son a collegiate education." This situation, to Chase, was "in direct hostility to the nature of a republic." Chase intended that Kenyon College be a corrective to this situation, that the college be accessible to men of whatever fortune.[33]

Denominational motives were national; what made the college-founding phenomenon regional was the large number of religious denominations. Because the West included immigrants from all sections of the Atlantic seaboard, as well as recent arrivals from Europe, the West had the widest and most diverse mix of American religious communities in the nation. In the South, several states were like Georgia, which had four colleges by 1860—a public university and three colleges founded by the three dominant denominations in the state, the Methodists, the Baptists, and the Presbyterians. Lack of denominational variety reduced the number of colleges founded. Also, the West had no tradition of an established church, while the remnants of established religion still played an important role in other regions.[34]

In this situation the state legislatures of the West encouraged denominational colleges, beginning in the middle 1820s. Prior to the mid-1820s, Old Northwest state legislators mostly chartered a few state universities. This early tendency resembled the structure of higher education in most Southern states, where state universities rather than private denominational colleges were emphasized. Until 1850 in South Carolina, in fact, state legislators refused to charter denominational colleges. State universities dominated the landscape of Southern higher education. But Western legislators in the 1820s shifted course. Ohio legislators began to charter denominational colleges; Indiana and Illinois legislators soon did likewise.[35]

From 1825, Western state legislators issued charters freely. In the 1830s, Thomas King described to his mother the course of study at his Chillicothe, Ohio, school. "I date my letter from Trinity college," he noted, as "that is the name Mr. Garrett has given it." The Ohio state legislators, King reported, had granted a charter so that Trinity College "should be enlarged at pleasure." In granting these charters without any financial aid, state legislators recognized that the state simply did not have the financial resources to support public higher education, the bureaucratic apparatus to oversee these institutions, or the educational expertise to manage them. Most antebellum Western state universities, including Ohio University, Miami University, and Indiana University, despite their "public" status, were run by religious denominations, usually Presbyterians, who packed the boards of trustees.[36] But soon politicians decided to be even less in control and let churches and local communities provide the financial support, decide where to locate a college, operate it daily, and take the risks besides. The Western states willingly accepted partnerships with religious denominations to help create civil society. State leaders did not abdicate their roles in guiding their states into the future, nor did they cynically maneuver to create that best government which governs least. Rather, they sought to contribute to the public good despite the limitations of their own power. They created institutions outside the authority of and not financially dependent on the state, yet complementary to the state's goals.

In most cases, state legislators placed few restrictions on the colleges. They often required that colleges be nonsectarian, which simply meant that students of any religious background or belief ought to be able to attend. Aside from this, state representatives exercised almost no oversight over the colleges beyond requiring them to meet certain capitalization requirements and avoid engaging in banking practices. The sole Western attempt to take away a collegiate charter, an attack on Oberlin because of its abolitionist character, failed.[37]

The presidents and professors at these Western colleges were like the settlers to the region—extremely diverse. Most of the founders and early leaders had spent most of their adult lives in the West. Timothy Smith argued that these Western colleges were indigenous institutions, and that the well-publicized efforts, for example, of the "Yale Band," Yale graduates who founded Illinois College, were not reflective of overall regional patterns. Smith was countering long-standing claims that Western colleges were primarily founded and led by New Englanders. Smith's findings, based on Illinois and Indiana, have more recently been buttressed by the work of D. Randall Gabrielse, who studied antebellum Michigan and Ohio colleges and found that their faculty members were primarily graduates of Ohio and Pennsylvania colleges. Overall, Western college faculty members, like the general population, represented a remarkable mixture of regional backgrounds.[38]

This Western structure of collegiate education did not go uncontested, however. Until 1843, each Western college sent out agents or a president who appealed for donations from individuals and churches in the Eastern states. Westerners began to inundate Easterners with appeal after appeal on behalf of a multitude of colleges. Some sought-after donors began to worry that some of these colleges were merely academies, or perhaps did not even exist. This doubt led to cynicism that hampered fund-raising efforts.

In this situation, a number of Western college presidents who ran Congregational and Presbyterian schools banded together and in 1843 founded the Society for the Promotion of Collegiate and Theological Education at the West (S.P.C.T.E.W.), commonly called the Western Education Society, to systematize collegiate aid solicitations in Eastern states. The organization would funnel Eastern monies to select Western schools. The college presidents expected that aid would increase, since Eastern donors would know that their money was going to a worthy cause. The membership would be comprised of Eastern donors; Easterners would control the Society. Thus constituted, the Western Education Society was an Eastern organization.[39]

The plan for the Western Education Society met with acclamation in Eastern states, where people believed that collegiate education in the West was chaotic. In New England, the presence of an established church, supported through taxation and governmental preference, had led to a slower pace of building colleges. Reverend Absalom Peters, a prominent leader of the American Home Missionary Society, told the Western Education Society that when their organization was founded, "A hundred beginnings had already been made" in the West. "But they were without concert.... we saw the necessity of an organization to harmonize the diverging and scattered action which was wasting itself in this impracticable way." Peters recognized that the Western colleges were founded not with any overarching plan, but as each locality and denomination desired. To the Western Education Society leaders, such a method was inefficient and undesirable. "The introduction of something like *system* into educational movements at the West," the first report of the Western Educational Society announced, "has met with a warm response in the East." The authors praised effective coordination, because "it is not very wonderful that many *attempts* should be made where but a single institution is needed."[40]

In 1845, the second report explicated the ideal plan for Western colleges. The model would be colonial New England, where, as early as 1644, the people of New Haven had supported Harvard College and delayed the beginning of Yale for decades. "Here was Puritan wisdom.

In the exercise of similar wisdom, this Society was organized." Eastern churches and donors would do better to support Western colleges "by giving a vigorous and permanent existence to a few, than by scattering their resources among a multitude that would inevitably conflict with each other, and entail upon all perpetual feebleness and inefficiency." The Society pledged to give money only to colleges well-established and locally supported: "By pursuing rigidly such a course, we hope to counteract in some measure the tendency to a reckless multiplication of ill projected and ill managed institutions." For these New Englanders, the fewer colleges in the West, the better. This theme continued and predominated in Western Education Society publications.[41]

With few exceptions, the Society aided Presbyterian and Congregational colleges with close ties to New England. Yet while the Western Education Society did succeed in supporting certain schools adequately, the goal of introducing a New England–style structure of higher education in the West went unfulfilled. While the Western Education Society may have slowed the pace of college founding among Presbyterians and Congregationalists in the West, these denominations made up only a small fraction of the Western religious landscape. Many other denominations operated without any knowledge of or concern about the Western Education Society. Townspeople clamored for colleges, and state legislators passed out the charters, with one exception.

A second force also worked against college proliferation, as leaders of the territory and state of Michigan followed an alternative model between 1817 and 1855. In 1817, the governor and judges of the Michigan Territory decided that education in Michigan should be controlled by a center of power at the territorial or state level. Soon after Michigan became a state, in 1837 the Michigan legislators founded the University of Michigan, which was supposed to provide all college degrees in the state. State political leaders mostly stifled efforts by religious denominations to obtain collegiate charters, but in 1854 the new Republican Party won the governorship as well as majority status in both halves of the legislature. Members of groups who advocated reform efforts such as antislavery, women's rights (including advocating a coeducational University of Michigan), and temperance supported the Republican Party, and some of these reformers were affiliated with denominational schools. James A. B. and Lucinda Hinsdale Stone, for example, of Kalamazoo College, were Michigan leaders against slavery and for women's rights. Hillsdale College was a center of antislavery sentiment in the state. The close connection between the Republican Party and the denominational colleges is exemplified by Hillsdale's president, Edmund Fairfield, who became vice-governor of Michigan. When the Republicans took office, they allowed for the charter of degree-granting denominational colleges, which then proliferated. By 1860 a structure of higher education that included decentralized control over numerous town-based denominational colleges had been achieved in Michigan and throughout the Western states.[42]

These numerous Western colleges were significant partly because having so many colleges in so many places broadened the opportunities for young people to attend them at a time when transportation was often both inconvenient and expensive. This landscape of higher education also provided the basis for a number of other differences that marked many Western colleges. Curriculum and extracurriculum—what was taught, how it was taught, and what else the college offered—further differentiated Western colleges from their Eastern and Southern counterparts. The manual labor movement described in the next chapter became a focal point of these differences.

2 / Manual Labor and the Producers

In 1838, Jonathan Going, the incoming president of the Granville Literary & Theological Institution, of Granville, Ohio, announced in his inaugural address that education was "naturally divided into three departments,—physical, intellectual, and moral." Going was not advancing a radical proposition. Other educators at this time, especially in the West, used the same language (sometimes adding a fourth category, manners, or the polite). They were articulating a growing belief that education meant more than mental training exclusively.[1]

The manual labor movement headlined this vision of education as more expansive than the classical curriculum of most American colleges. A manual labor system operated with the belief that work and schooling were best intertwined, and that all students should work. Though American educators implemented manual labor training as part of the educative process as early as 1785, the origins of the national manual labor movement after 1825 came partially from the ideas of European educators Johann Heinrich Pestalozzi and Emanuel von Fellenberg. Pestalozzi and Fellenberg, however, used their manual labor educational methods to reinforce class structures and social hierarchies. American educators, more interested in the possibilities of manual labor to provide social mobility and benefit a republican society, only loosely based their schools upon these European models and created a largely indigenous system in the process.[2]

It would be going too far to describe manual labor as being hostile to the market revolution and anticapitalistic. Paul Goodman was probably most accurate when he wrote that the manual labor movement evinced "a deep disquiet" with an economic system that valued even humans in monetary terms. Not coincidentally, manual labor was closely allied with immediate abolitionism and strongly tied to a "Christian republicanism" that gave the egalitarian and reformist nature of manual labor a moral dimension that is otherwise obscured.[3]

Manual labor education started in the United States in the mid-1820s in Maine, Massachusetts, and New York, and quickly spread elsewhere. In the early 1830s, the Oneida Institute of Science and Industry in upstate New York was the best-known manual labor school, and it was from here that Connecticut native Theodore Dwight Weld emerged as the chief propagandist for the system. Before he became a prominent abolitionist and advocate for women's rights, Weld worked for years on behalf of manual labor. He traveled widely and assisted schools setting up the program. In 1833, Weld authored an influential report from the Society for Promoting Manual Labor in Literary Institutions, which served as the central document of the movement.[4]

Weld's basic argument was that the mind and body are connected: thus, "the best condition of the mental powers cannot be found *permanently* connected with any other than the best condition of the bodily powers." He mustered dozens of testimonials from educators of the period, all of whom said that the health of many of their students was seriously impaired because the students took no regular exercise. For example, President Partridge, of Mississippi's Jefferson College, attested that "so many of our most promising youth lose their health by the time they are prepared to enter on the grand theatre of active and useful life, and either prematurely die or linger out a *comparatively useless and miserable existence*." The Report presented going to college as an incredible health hazard. Even worse, study without exercise "effeminates the mind," argued Weld, and "exercise is indispensable to summon out the *utmost possibility* of mental effort." Manual labor would take away idle hours of listlessness, build up "habits of activity and industry," and prevent a caste society in which the "laboring classes become hewers of wood and drawers of water for the educated." Weld condemned gymnastics as "*dangerous*" and "*unnatural*," but praised manual labor for promoting "habits of industry," "independence of character," "originality," and "all the manlier features of character." Weld hoped to banish "those absurd distinctions in society which make the occupation of an individual the standard of his worth." Put everyone to work, three hours a day, in agricultural and mechanical pursuits, and "[I]nstead of being driven asunder by jealousies, and smothered animosities, they approach each other with looks of kindness, and form a compact, based upon republican equality, and interchange of mutual offices of courtesy and kindness."[5] Weld's report circulated widely and inspired many schools to adopt manual labor.

Oberlin College exemplifies how the manual labor system functioned. Oberlin was one of the most dedicated manual labor colleges, and John J. Shipherd and Philo Stewart, the founders, intended Oberlin to be a manual labor school. This plan was abundantly clear from the opening advertisement that appeared in prominent newspapers of 1833. "The Manual Labor Department will receive unusual attention," the notice read, "being not (as is too common), regarded as an unimportant appendage to the literary department; but systematized and incorporated with it." Shipherd and Stewart criticized other, less complete, manual labor programs, in which work was optional, which tended to distinguish wealthy and poor students. At Oberlin all students would work, normally four hours each day.[6]

Students did not lack for opportunities for work. Forested areas needed to be cleared, stumps grubbed. Students erected college buildings and built roads. Delazon Smith went to Oberlin during its first years and graduated in 1837, only to publish a bitter indictment of the college, entitled *A History of Oberlin, or New Lights of the West*, more popularly known as *Oberlin Unmasked*. As opposed to much of the rhetoric that surrounded manual labor, which presented the work as ennobling and invigorating, as well as teaching a useful trade, Smith wrote that "Nearly all the labor since this Institution was first established, has been chopping, logging and burning brush; and this too, a great portion of the year, *ankle deep in mud and water!*" He had a point. Especially early on, the work was often not glamorous and not particularly well suited for teaching students a trade. Yet the students were physically active, defrayed their educational costs, and built the very college they attended.[7]

At Oberlin, the definition of manual labor expanded as the college developed. Sundry chores and tasks had to be completed to keep the college functioning. By no means was this a rigidly equal system. Some jobs paid better than others. Also, while both males and females worked at coeducational manual labor schools, the jobs of women and men overlapped only somewhat. As in most households of the time, Oberlin females washed, ironed, sewed, mended, cooked, cleaned, and scrubbed while the males normally worked at outside jobs, particularly on the college farm, though men also cleaned Ladies' Hall, waited tables, and prepared food in the kitchen.[8]

The 500-acre farm at Oberlin provided a large portion of the sustenance of both educators and students. Livestock included horses, oxen, cows, bulls, sheep, and hogs. The primary crop was wheat, which students planted on 45 acres in 1838. Some land, of course, was pasture, while the Oberlinites used other acreage to grow "oats, potatoes, peas, beans, buckwheat, rye and corn," as well as apple and peach trees. The Oberlin students performed all of the myriad tasks that farms require: they plowed and harvested, they milked the cows and built fences to keep the livestock handy. In short, the Oberlin farm was a sizeable and working farm that provided food for the college and employment for students.[9]

The only thing the farm was not was profitable, as was universally discovered, and manual labor systems declined precipitously in the middle and late 1830s, though Western colleges tended to cling longest to the system. The trustees of Hanover College in Indiana, for example, explained to the state legislature in 1834 that they were fully aware that manual labor programs were not "very lucrative," and yet they justified their extensive manual labor operations on the grounds that they were necessary as "a preservation of health, . . . a means of invigorating the mind," and "a most effectual safeguard to morals." They also emphasized how "antirepublican" an expensive education was and promised, through manual labor, "to throw open the door of science to all talented and enterprising young men whatever may be their circumstances." An ideal of providing nearly universal access to education sustained a Western commitment to manual labor.[10]

At Oberlin, for example, manual labor went through a long and gradual decline. By the middle 1830s, administrators were unable to furnish every student with labor; in the late 1830s the daily work requirement dropped from four hours to two. As late as 1845, college officials still insisted that manual labor was fundamental to the college, but during the 1840s the leaders of Oberlin discarded and reconfigured the system in a number of ways. Administrators gave each student a plot of land, later rented the land to farmers who agreed to hire Oberlin students as laborers, and, finally, leased the land perpetually, as the land could not be sold under the original agreement of the Oberlin colony.[11] For students, the decline of manual labor was gradual; as employment on the campus lessened, students increasingly looked for employment beyond the college. For girls, housework was one possibility. More commonly, however, both male and female students took jobs as teachers. Soon Oberlin, like other colleges, sent out hundreds of students each winter to teach school, usually for three months.

By adopting manual labor programs, colleges were challenging the existing curriculum and structure of higher education, which was a classical education. A classical education emphasized language training, Greek and Latin, in order to allow students to translate and read ancient thinkers and writers such as Tacitus, Homer, Livy, Horace, Plato, and Thucydides. In the late 1700s, following American independence from British colonial rule, Americans began to discuss changes to the classical curriculum. Two deviations came in the 1820s from the University of Virginia, where students could choose from eight different courses of study, and from Harvard, where students could partially replace study of a classical language with a modern language. In response to these changes and calls for a more practical and American system of education, the Yale faculty defended a classical education in the Yale Report of 1828.[12]

The Yale Report was by no means a reactionary document. The authors agreed that "our present plan of education admits of improvement. We are aware that the system is imperfect." The real question for the Yale faculty was whether the situation called for modest reforms or wholesale changes. In part, the faculty argued, the answer depended on what a collegiate education was supposed to provide. "The two great points to be gained in intellectual culture," they stated, "are the *discipline* and the *furniture* of the mind." The college years were a time for "the training of the powers of the mind." At college one learned mental skills, including "demonstrative reasoning," "induction," "taste" in literature, and the arts of thinking, speaking, and writing. Students could apply these mental skills to anything they might choose, but one applied these skills only after passage through a collegiate course of study.[13]

The authors understood that many Americans could not afford the education the Yale Report recommended. "Many, for want of time and pecuniary resources, must be content with a partial course." The Yale faculty was not against such an education. "A defective education is better than none." But all should recognize that an education other than a classical education "is an imperfection, arising from the necessity of the case. A partial course of study, must inevitably give a partial education." For these professors, a classical education provided the standard that no other educational system could match.[14]

For the rest of the antebellum period, most Eastern colleges retained a classical curriculum, and most Southern colleges did as well. The

Southern interest in the classics drew added strength because many Southerners who supported slavery drew connections between the American South and ancient Greece and wanted Greek in the curriculum. Southern college leaders also defended a classical education as a requisite characteristic of being a gentleman. Greek and Latin were languages of the master class.[15]

In the West, people liked manual labor, sometimes because they wanted their children to learn a trade and stay healthy. In 1836, Micaiah Fairfield, a printer who lived in Troy, Ohio, sent his fifteen-year-old son, Edmund, to Granville with a letter for the president. "I expect him to work in the coopers-shop," wrote Micaiah, referring to Edmund. Beyond that assignment, though, "I have no choice in his employment if he has good exercise & regular employment." Micaiah did, however, want to make sure that Edmund worked enough hours in the cooper's shop. "I insist on his laboring four hours a day that he may learn his trade & work to advantage afterwords." Fairfield wanted his son to receive sufficient exercise and be trained in a trade that would bring gainful employment.[16]

Within four years, however, Fairfield's priorities had shifted slightly. His sons were interested in transferring to Oberlin, and Fairfield wrote to Oberlin to inquire about the manual labor program there. "I have two sons who wish to get an education for the Ministry," Fairfield wrote. "I wish them to pay their board in their own labor if possible." Fairfield had heard that "you can all get work in the cooper's shop. . . . I would prefer coopering to anything else." Fairfield suggested a compromise, however, should work as a cooper be unavailable. He added that "Edmund is a pretty good printer. Perhaps he might work in your printing office. That I deem less healthy employment than coopering, but usually commands higher wages. I think they will both come if they can get employment in a coopers shop."[17] No longer did Fairfield desire to train his sons for a manual labor occupation. Manual labor, though, remained important for two reasons: first, to defray educational costs; second, and more importantly, for their health, as Fairfield wanted his son Edmund to work at the less lucrative but more vigorous job of coopering.

It turned out that the manual labor experience was not wasted on Edmund. When he became president of Hillsdale College in Michigan in 1848, the house he was provided by the college was, in his words, "a weather-beaten frame building, innocent of paint . . . . A few of the clapboards hung by a single nail. The whole house would have been dear at a hundred dollars. Fortunately I had worked my way through college by mechanical work, so, besides nailing up the loose boards,

I proceeded in my manual labor hours to whitewash the 'President's House'!"[18]

Western parents and students alike often demanded that colleges furnish students with opportunities for physical exertion, and they saw the Western colleges as the best places to receive this kind of education. In 1846 a farmer from Clark County, Ohio, wrote to Oberlin inquiring about admission for his nineteen-year-old son. "My own opinion," he confided, "is that the physical education ought to be attended to as well as the mental, and we have had some hints that this is a part of your plan." Some parents specified what physical exertion or labor their child should do. In 1849, Sophia Noel of Fort Wayne, Indiana, inquired about her son, who had been at Hanover for two months. She wrote that her son had always been active, "and will need as all children do, outdoor exercise, that I presume he can have and does. choping his wood, and do-ing other things." In 1854, Hoosier James Crawford, of Sullivan County, sent his son to Hanover with instructions to the faculty that "I should like him to board so far from the college that he would be compelled to take sufficient exercise and compelled to rise early."[19]

Some students expressly sought manual labor education because they believed they could thereby protect their health. In 1837, for example, Franklin Merrill inquired about the possibility of coming to the West for college. Merrill had been a college student in Middlebury, Vermont, and was dissatisfied, in part, because of the *"Want of proper exercise."* Mer-rill explained that he had no opportunity for exercise beyond walking, and that many of his fellow students complained of "declining" health, "so that probaly many after haveing completed there Studies will not be fit for usefullness. This to me, appears to be a very important consider-ation. . . . The *church* and *times demand* a *pious, holy, devoted,* and *active ministry."* In 1846, Jared Baldwin inquired about admission to Oberlin. He explained that he had heard that Oberlin operated "on the laboring system which suits my situation, and Inclination, for I am of an active habit and require some active exercise each day in order that I may keep up a healthy action both Mentally and Physically."[20]

The emphasis on physical education is not remarkable when one considers the lives of Western educators, who often had to meet intense physical demands. These educators were not frail, worn-out men who could no longer stand the rigors of the circuit rider or itinerant preacher. The Western college professors were often hardy young men. Sarah King visited Kenyon College in the early 1830s. She wrote that Charles P. Mc-Ilvaine, the president of Kenyon and Episcopal Bishop of Ohio, "armed with an axe, is vigorously cutting away at sundry old stumps." Students were startled by these presidents doing such work. Elijah Evan Edwards arrived as a student at Indiana Asbury for the first time in 1846 and went to look for the president, Matthew Simpson, to give Simpson a letter of introduction. As Edwards wrote in his diary, he found Simpson at work: "He had a saw in his hands and was in his shirt sleeves and did not look at all like a College President. I did not believe he was, and so asked him if he could tell me where I would find President Simpson." Sometimes the tools found indoor use, as in 1854, when Edmund O. Hovey told about two Wabash College students who would not come out of a room and forcibly shut the door. When Professor Caleb Mills told the boys to open the door and the boys disobeyed, Mills broke down the door with an axe. When Hovey wrote to Charles White, an Easterner, about coming to Wabash College as president, he admitted that not everyone believed White could do the job: "Rev. David Merrill of Urbanna . . . says you are doubtless well qualified for the 'inside work' of college; but has his doubts whether you will succeed as well *outside*. Thinks you have too much *refinement* for a western college."[21]

Enthusiasm for physical exertion was obviously tied to ideas about masculinity. When Charles B. Storrs became the president of Western Reserve College in 1831, he told the audience assembled for his inaugural address that an important question for the school was "*whether mere diversion and gymnastic exercise ought not, in academic discipline, to give place to systematic manual labor.*" Storrs stood on behalf of manual labor. "A system of manual labor, well arranged," he argued, "is not only better adapted to preserve and confirm the health . . . . It will contribute to give the character a manliness, a consistency, an enterprising turn." The founder of Hanover College in Indiana explained that one reason he started manual labor in the 1830s at Hanover was that "it was urged that men of more than ordinary nerve and muscle were needed as pioneers of the church, and that consequently those who had been early thrown upon their own resources and had learned to bear hardness as good Soldiers, were just the men for the field."[22]

In other words, manual labor would help give students the physical vigor and character the West would require. At Michigan Central College in 1848 the state examiner heard the students declaim and then recorded that they "showed originality of thought and manliness of bearing found only in institutions of the West." In 1853, Western educator Jonathan B. Turner denounced University of Michigan president Henry Tappan for introducing Prussian educational ideas. Rather, Turner exclaimed, "true manhood" was the goal of the educator, which meant offering students the opportunity to learn a trade. Manual labor satisfied regional demands for this kind of manhood.[23]

Parents echoed this connection between vocational education and masculinity. In April 1834, Charles Larrabee sent his son to the Baptist Granville Literary Institute and wrote to President John Pratt, "I am anxious you should make a man of him from this time out. . . . Should you be able to learn him some mechanical trade, I should be much pleased." By January 1835, Larrabee grew more direct about his philosophy of education. "You informed me when last here that Charles was learning the coopers trade. I wish it distinctly understood that he was sent to & he remains, with you," Larrabee emphasized:

> . . . under the surety of being learned some manual labour trade. I conceive it as great a wrong as can be done to children, to bring them up without learning them the use the Creator made their hands for, and that it is a gross imposition upon the mind, faculties & abilities of men to be brought up without any knowledge or experience of actual labor. No man ought to be considered but half taught, but half a man, however great his acquirements from books, who knows nothing of manual labor by experience, & none should be considered capable or worthy of public confidence or trust, short of this experience.[24]

Larrabee, in both letters, assigned John Pratt, the president of Granville, with the responsibility of making Larrabee's son into a man. And "half" of being a man, for Larrabee, meant knowing "manual labor by experience." Manual labor was essential even for men who would not labor manually as part of their career. The "public" should not accept men as leaders who had not performed manual labor. Larrabee's comments exemplified an anti-elitist belief in the dignity of labor and the idea that all classes should know manual labor, even if they went on to other employments. Labor made one worthy of the public trust.

In the West, manual labor remained fashionable even after it had disappeared from higher education elsewhere in the United States. In 1854, the president of Antioch College knew his Cincinnati audience when he admonished during a lecture that "We must pay far more attention to the health of the students." He claimed that the faculty believed in manual labor; the professors "encourage manual labor in every practicable way; and if a liberal public, or a liberal individual, would give us land for agricultural, or even for horticultural purposes . . . we promise them that the old injunction, *to till the ground and dress it*, shall not be forgotten." Numerous Eastern schools, such as Amherst, Dartmouth, and Williams, had applied manual labor ideas to their existing institutions, and manual labor was not central to the educational process. When the manual labor system proved financially unremunerative, educators at these schools simply shed the system. By 1838, two young men applied to a Western college "for the reason that there is no Manual Labor College in New England."[25]

Nonplussed by manual labor, Easterners thought of other ways to maintain the health of their students, especially through gymnastics, which appealed especially to the upper class. Thomas Jefferson believed that gymnastics promoted good health and would be a necessary component of military education. Thus, from its beginning in the 1820s, the University of Virginia offered boxing and fencing, as well as "single-stick," "quarter-staff," and "broad-sword" sparring. Along with these combative exercises, students at Virginia worked with "parallel bars, ladders and ropes." Gymnastics rarely extended further south from Virginia, although other Virginia schools had gymnastics. At Randolph-Macon College, a lithograph on a diploma from 1860 showed parallel bars, rings, and other bars in the view of the campus. Georgetown students favored handball, but also fenced, boxed, performed chin-ups, and threw weights. Other schools that brought in gymnastics by the end of the antebellum period included Princeton, Yale, Dartmouth, Middlebury, Bowdoin, and Amherst.[26]

William Gardiner Hammond, an undergraduate at Amherst in the 1840s, described frequent games of wicket. At the gym, where he often exercised, Hammond "tried the circular swing" and "threw loggerheads." Hammond's awareness of class differences was never more acute than when he attended a "great cattle show and fair in the village," where he was astonished by the people who came in from the countryside. Hammond mingled with these people "and watched them, ungainly in form, uncouth in dress, without a spark of true nobility about them, their countenances marked only by sordid meanness or beastly passion, and as devoid of mind or soul as their very cattle."[27] Hammond displayed none of the connection to the laboring classes that manual labor programs were designed to yield.

For a time, manual labor programs were popular in the South. Yet while some Southern colleges claim manual labor origins, the actual number of colleges that sustained manual labor programs was low. Some schools with manual labor components of the curriculum ended manual labor before the school became a college. For example, Howard University (Alabama), Furman University, and the University of Richmond never had manual labor at the collegiate level. Rather, they were successor institutions, sometimes many years later, in a different location, and in name only, of failed seminaries or academies that had been based upon manual labor.[28]

Even at colleges with manual labor programs, these programs were usually short-lived. In Kentucky, Centre College ran two farms, which students called "Do Little" and "Do Less." The program soon ended. At Emory and Oglethorpe, trustees discontinued manual labor within a year. Mercer and Wake Forest, both Baptist institutions, were more dedicated to manual labor. Wake Forest, in particular, revealed elite Southern attitudes toward manual labor. There, manual labor was controversial from the start. Supporters of the program recognized that opponents associated manual labor with degradation in their slave-based society. The *Baptist Weekly Journal*, in 1832, even went so far as to declare that "One of the grand objects of the institution is to overcome southern habits and prejudices against manual labor and to promote habits of economy and industry." The experiment at Wake Forest and at Mercer lasted longer than at other Southern schools, but even at these schools manual labor disappeared after five years' time. In Kentucky, Cumberland College began a manual labor program in the late 1820s that lasted at least until 1832, but failed shortly thereafter. At Presbyterian Davidson College, students, led by the most wealthy among them, vigorously subverted the manual labor program through pranks and destruction of property, including taking apart a wagon and hanging the parts in a tree. Manual labor began there in 1837; trustees gave in four years later.[29]

At Emory and Henry, located in the mountains of western Virginia, this Methodist school was organized on the manual labor plan in 1838, with the requirement that all students work three hours each day on the farm. Yet by 1841 the trustees scaled back the necessary hours to two each day, and the following year they eliminated the work requirement altogether. Emory and Henry, at its start, drew its students from the mountainous and immediate area near the college, which hosted a farming population sympathetic to manual labor programs. These farmers were more likely to support the college and send their sons there if it had a manual labor program than if it did not. But as Emory and Henry flourished, the college began drawing students from all parts of the South. Many of these students had little acquaintance with manual labor, and coming from areas more heavily dominated by slavery, they associated manual labor with degradation. Rather than create social distinctions at the college between those students who performed manual labor and those who did not, Emory and Henry ultimately abolished its manual labor program in 1848, a victim of a dominant Southern culture that was uncomfortable with the implications of manual labor.[30]

In 1839, South Carolinian Robert S. Bailey visited Jubilee College in Illinois. The head of Jubilee, Philander Chase (who had founded Jubilee following his ouster from Kenyon), toured Bailey around the college. Bailey was particularly interested in the banks of coal that Chase was mining and mentioned encountering "a young man with a cart load of the coal." After the man passed, Chase explained that the young coal miner "was qualifying himself for the ministry, and would soon be able to take orders, and that although we saw him so employed, he was nevertheless a gentleman that possessed talents of the first order."[31] Chase, familiar with elite Southern culture, knew what Bailey and his readers would presume about a student who mined coal, thus Chase stated explicitly that "although" a student performed manual labor, "he was nevertheless" a gentleman with talent.

Far more popular and in keeping with a Southern culture of honor, in which Southern college students prepared to become gentlemen, was military drill. The connections between military drill and gentlemanly status are mostly implicit, although the Georgetown Cadets adhered to "a code of gentlemanly conduct." The earliest prominent Southern example of military instruction was the University of Virginia. Thomas Jefferson recommended that the University of Virginia include military drill for its students, and when the University opened, the Board of Trustees required in 1824 that all students perform military drill weekly, on Saturdays, under the direction of a military instructor. Military instruction, companies, and drill, both student-led and instructor-led, characterized many Southern colleges, especially during and after the 1840s. Washington College and the Virginia Military Institute worked together to offer their students uniformed military drill and military engineering. One historian, who did not distinguish between colleges and academies, found ninety-six antebellum military institutions in the South, as opposed to only fifteen such schools in the North. Some of these schools, such as the Virginia Military Institute (1839) and the South Carolina Military Academy (1842), were state-funded institutions. Others had variations of student-organized voluntary drill companies, some college-supported, others with various degrees of faculty and college opposition. The historian of Furman University found that while the faculty in 1856

approved formation of a military company, it was decidedly "not en-
thusiastic." The faculty insisted that students have parental permission,
that the faculty receive a roll of the company twice each year, and that
the company members promise "to deliver up their arms upon demand
of any faculty member." An earlier example of faculty concerns comes
from the University of Georgia, which had a tradition of student militia
activity dating at least from 1812. At one point, the trustees and faculty
were alarmed when the Georgia governor sent students a "wagon load of
rifles," in violation of the rule that no students should have weapons. The
faculty confiscated the firearms and sent them back to the governor.[32]

The rhetoric surrounding military education partially resembled the
ideas concerning manual labor. Students extolled military drill as an opportunity for healthful exercise, and as a means of building character.
But military aspects of educational life had other virtues, as well, according to their proponents. A Citadel professor extolled "the habits of order,
self-dependence, and restraint that they engender; the sense of duty and
responsibility they inculcate; the manly bearing they impart." The 1855
announcement of the opening of Western Military Academy in Tennessee explained that "military exercises and military discipline . . . promotes
three great moral principles—*obedience, subordination,* and *method*—the
elements that secure deference to authority, fidelity to law, the performance
of obligations, the observance of every duty and adherence to all the great
principles of society." Southerners particularly liked military training because they believed such training would encourage discipline, which contemporaries claimed was lacking in many Southern males.[33]

Another virtue of military groups, according to proponents, was their
tendency to make students equal, especially through uniforms. In 1836,
at Georgetown, students formed the College Cadets. "The ordinary college dress was adopted as the basic uniform. The trimming of the pan-
taloons with red braid, the addition of a red sash and a start gave the
proper distinction." At other schools, uniforms were prescribed even
when the school offered no military training. At the beginning of the
University of Alabama, all students wore "a frock coat of dark blue cloth,
single-breasted, with standing collar, ornamented on each side with a
gilt star, a single row of gilt buttons in front, and six buttons on the back.
A black stock and a black hat with narrow brim" helped to complete the
student's dress.[34] Such uniforms, however, while they may have made the
students equal to each other as gentlemen and men of honor, severely
distinguished the uniformed students from nonstudents. By way of com-

parison, students who worked at manual labor were made not only equal to each other, but equal to other laborers.

In the Northeast, some colleges had military programs. West Point, of course, was a military academy. New Hampshire and Vermont schools also had a military component. At Dartmouth, in 1845, the faculty abolished the Dartmouth Phalanx, a student military company, "because it was deemed too devoted to spirits." In Norwich, Vermont, a West Point graduate named Alden Partridge founded a military academy in 1819 that grew in 1834 into Norwich University, and which produced many graduates who would go on to lead other, especially Southern, military schools. At Norwich, all students studied military science, and took part in military drill, supplied with muskets, bayonets, and cannon by the state of Vermont. Norwich University made its commitments explicit in the 1850 catalog, in which it explained that the University intended "to train, improve and discipline the body, so that it may be able to cooperate with the mind to execute its highest and best purposes." Military drill "is an agreeable relaxation to the student, strengthens the frame and fits him for his mental studies, whilst those habits of prompt, strict obedience and regularity, which always distinguish the soldier, are acquired."[35] Still, in comparison to schools in the South, those in New England and elsewhere in the East adopted military companies and curricula at a slow rate.

Almost all Western colleges eschewed military drill and gymnastics.[36] In the West, a cultural region dominated by middle-class values, manual labor schools suited a regional predisposition toward production. Gymnastics was not only not productive, it seemed effete in comparison to manual labor. And while military drill carried requisite masculinity, it too was nonproductive, and cultivated both an elite status and physical aggression. Southern masculinity and violence went hand in hand, while in the West the tools of manhood were the ax and the plow, rather than the musket or the dueling pistol.

It is not difficult to see how the ethos that supported manual labor, in which students worked, often on a farm, to support their studies, could be extended into a program in which the farm itself became part of academic study. The advent of scientific agriculture was most prominent in the West at Farmers' College, located outside Cincinnati. The founder of Farmers' was Freeman Cary, born in 1810 in southwestern Ohio. In 1831 he graduated from Miami University and soon established the Pleasant Hill Academy in Hamilton County, Ohio. Cary's academy prospered, and by the middle 1840s Cary began to think about expanding his academy into a full-fledged college.[37]

The type of college Cary envisioned was one that would be useful to farmers. Years earlier, in 1832, Cary delivered an address before the Hamilton County Agricultural Society in which he argued that the Americans needed schools that provided an agricultural education. Farmers must go to school so that they could be useful citizens, ones familiar with the governmental ways of a republic, who also knew how to farm successfully. In the 1840s, as Cary considered what sort of college to establish, he returned to these ideas of agricultural education. Therefore, when Ohio state legislators chartered the college, they chartered Farmers' College.[38]

Between 1854 and 1856, Freeman Cary acquired a farm of 100 acres near the college and built an experimental laboratory on the grounds. Students and faculty conducted tests upon different strains of wheat, other grasses, vegetables, and fruit trees. Cary wrote that from the beginning, he had attempted to supply students with an education "eminently practical." The agricultural department, claimed Cary, would offer "everything calculated to render the business of farming more flourishing, prosperous, and productive." The teachers at Farmers' would educate students about mathematics in agriculture, soil management, "zoology, entomology, and natural history in general, political economy, and many other branches."[39]

In 1856 Cary began to publish a monthly serial, *Cincinnatus*, which served as an agricultural journal and official organ for Farmers' College. In this publication, Cary explained his educational philosophy and the innovations of Farmers' College. "Harvard, Yale, and Dartmouth," Cary wrote, represented the standard collegiate structures in the United States. The founders of these schools had modeled them after English schools, and these Eastern schools stood "for the education of the few, the students of the learned professions." Cary thought that Farmers' College represented a break with the past. "We propose," Cary announced, an educational system "less scholastic, less monkish; not atheistic, nor yet ecclesiastic; not Prussian, not French, not royal, not aristocratic, but truly and symmetrically American, Christian, industrial and universal." During the 1856 dedication of Polytechnic Hall, Freeman Cary told those assembled, "We trust that it is the mission of American institutions . . . to enlarge the idea of a University, until it shall embrace the education of men for every honorable calling and pursuit."[40]

Cary broke with the past when he argued that scientific agriculture should be a standard part of collegiate education and American universities should provide vocational education. Cary saw Farmers' as an American college, not derivative of Old World influences, but one that met New World needs with indigenous educational ideas. Cary did not think of Farmers' as Western, but clearly the West provided an environment in which such a college could be founded.

Cary pictured his college as a building block of the nation. "America is now teaching the world a lesson with regard to popular sovereignty and man's inalienable rights," wrote Cary, who maintained that "there must be a lifting up of the industrial classes to a new position and placing them in a better relation to manhood and to humanity than they have ever occupied." Farmers' College would satisfy the promise of dignity and social mobility for all that Cary believed stood at the heart of the American system.[41]

The connections between manual labor and scientific agriculture are most explicit in the creation of Western College in Iowa, a school founded by United Brethren. The United Brethren were already strongly in favor of manual labor, having started a program of manual labor earlier in the 1850s at Otterbein University in Ohio. An 1857 explanation, from Solomon Weaver, the founder and first president of Western College, laid out the situation clearly. He acknowledged that "Manual Labor Colleges have been pronounced by high authority one of the humbugs of the age." Most schools had given up their programs twenty years earlier, and he understood why people might wonder why Western College would embrace manual labor. The answer, which included the fact that the college owned extensive and fertile farmland, was that "A Professor of Agriculture and Agricultural Chemistry has been employed. . . . It is designed to make the farm a model farm—to conduct it in a systematic manner, and to make it not merely a place where students will be furnished work to eke out a subsistence, but where they will be taught both the theory and practice of scientific agriculture." Students working on the farm would be "testing the advantages of different relation of crops—the comparative value of the various manures, both organic and inorganic, to different crops—the best manner of applying fertilizers, and so forth; and students will be particularly instructed in the best methods of conducting farm experiments so as to make them profitable, and to aid in perfecting a *Science of Agriculture*." Beyond this, an "Analytical Laboratory will be connected with the farm where students can be taught Analytic Chemistry, and especially the application of Chemistry to Agriculture." And to boot, every professor had to labor alongside the students. "All connected with the College must work. No Professor or

Teacher will be employed in any department, who is unwilling to work, and who does not work." The notion that each student should "labor to promote physical health, and thereby sharpen his mental powers, is just as applicable to the teacher, and will be treated accordingly."[42]

Western College's effort represented a self-conscious evolution of manual labor into scientific agriculture, which would soon be taken up in the following decades at state universities, especially the land-grant colleges founded following the Morrill Act of 1862. The evolution of scientific curricula and schools from their origins in the middle of the nineteenth century are convoluted, as Roger Geiger has explained. The point here is that manual labor ideas were easily transferable, especially through scientific agriculture, to scientific study.[43]

Western colleges reflected regional values as they emphasized this new educational profile. In 1847, Samuel Miller, a professor at Princeton Theological Seminary, recognized that the plans for agricultural education at Farmers' College represented an educational innovation he believed best suited for Westerners. Easterners, he argued, would not be attracted because they "have been altogether unused to any thing of the kind, & . . . are so much the slaves of old habits." Farmers', he mused, perhaps would "better suit the robust, active, & new & original forms of construction in everything." Easterners would remain attached to their existing educational ways, according to Miller. Farmers' would succeed because the Westerners were open to new ideas.[44]

Miller was not the only person who thought the regional ethos of the West was built around robust activity and originality. Timothy Flint, a Cincinnati student of Western culture, noticed that Westerners displayed "a vigor, an energy, a recklessness of manner and form, but a racy freshness of matter, which smacks strongly of our peculiar character and position." In 1840, Lewis Clarke, a seminary student at Andover in Massachusetts, wrote to his brother in Ohio that Lyman Beecher, of Lane Seminary in Cincinnati, had come to Andover for a few days. Beecher encouraged the Andover students to serve as ministers in the West, and Clarke confessed, "I have sometimes been half sorry I did not go to Lane Sem. instead of coming here—This is the better place for study:— that for making active, efficient men." Calvin Fletcher, in Indianapolis in 1823, wrote to his brother in New York that "People here are vastly different from N.Y. or N.E. . . . They are bold and independant in their sentiments. . . . A lawyer here must become a good advocate or speaker in public. In your country any man can be a good lawyer without saying a word." Less approvingly, New Englander Charles Peabody visited Ohio in 1850 and wrote in his diary that he liked "the frank, wide-awake, stirring spirit" he found there. "But this jumping and twitching at trifles, and going off half cocked without anything in but powder, I disapprove of entirely." Peabody framed the differences between the inhabitants of the two regions as analogous to the differences between an ox and a horse. "A Yankee takes every thing coolly and sits down and calculates the exact issue of his plans and projects . . . But the Buckeye dives into things with all his might, and begins to pull and haul, very much like a fractious horse hitched to a heavy stone." When all was said and done, according to Peabody, the Yankee was more productive, but the Buckeye made "a greater fuss and more splendid flourish of trumpets." A college student in Ohio distinguished between Pennsylvania and the West. "I tell you what," he wrote to a friend, "the Ohioans learn faster, live faster, arive faster, & die faster than Pennsylvanians." Peabody agreed: "Every thing is high pressure out here."[45] The themes were constant: in the East, people emphasized stability, laws, thought; the West was characterized by restless vigor, independence, action.

The lasting appeal of manual labor and, ultimately, scientific agriculture, and the willingness to alter the traditions of classical education, came out of a Western regional culture built around an egalitarian producer-culture masculinity that emphasized action and originality. The colleges were affected by these traits, but so was the broader population. Abraham Lincoln understood the region's values, and his rail-splitting image (the lawyer skillful with an axe) drew perfectly upon these deepseated regional commitments.

Just as the manual labor system opened up the opportunity to go to college to young people without much money, collegiate coeducation—the opening of student ranks to both males and females—represented a break with educational norms. The Western openness to collegiate coeducation illustrates the importance of usefulness as a regional priority, and is the topic of the next chapter.

3 / Coeducation and Usefulness

In 1860, J. H. Fairchild, Oberlin professor and soon-to-be president, prepared a lecture for a gathering of Oberlin graduates. Commenting on what Oberlin had meant during its few decades of existence, Fairchild declared, "Something has been done in the way of *popularizing education*, and adapting the style of education institutions to Western society and Western wants. The mistake has sometimes been made, of attempting to transplant Eastern educational systems, the growth of Eastern thought and social forces, without any modifications, to the West." Fairchild disparaged attempts to build "reproductions" of Eastern schools in the West as similar to trying to cultivate "Eastern fruit" in different soil. "These Eastern schools are the growth of the society in which they exist. A successful Western school must have a similar connection with Western society." In Fairchild's view, "Oberlin was the pioneer in a system of higher education at the West. This system is indigenous to the soil, and has shown its vitality in a vigorous growth." Other Western schools, many founded or staffed by Oberlinites, were "modeled upon the same general plan," continued Fairchild. "If the system be not adapted to Western society, the discovery will soon be made; for it is to be tested upon a wide scale."[1]

As is well known, in the 1830s the Oberlin Collegiate Institute in Ohio became the first college to school men and women together. In succeeding decades, collegiate coeducation flourished elsewhere, so that by 1860 over two dozen coeducational colleges operated in Western states, while no coeducational colleges existed in New England or the South. What would eventually become the norm in American higher education began in the Western states and for decades remained almost exclusively a Western phenomenon. As Fairchild argued, this origin and growth in the West was not an accident, but reflected a regional identity and values at odds with the prevailing norms in higher education. Collegiate coeducation radically departed from existing traditions in higher education, both American and European, where the medieval and monastic origins of the university precluded women from study. In these Western states, the forces that promoted coeducation included the liberality of granting charters and the marginality of many denominations that received charters. Members of small, usually rural, denominations were more egalitarian, practical, anti-elitist, and evangelical, and their gender ideals did not emphasize separate spheres or single-sex education. They manifested their producer-cultural orientation by explicitly invoking usefulness as a priority, a primary impetus toward coeducation. Coeducation represented a willingness to experiment, and Westerners were proud of their lack of strictures. They wanted their colleges to serve Western needs.

Collegiate coeducation was not accidental. As John J. Shipherd explained the principles of Oberlin at its founding in a *Circular* of 1834, the school sought "the elevation of female character, bringing within the reach of the misjudged and neglected sex, all the instructive privileges which hitherto have unreasonably distinguished the leading sex from theirs." Oberlin would school men and women together in the same classrooms. Shipherd did not wander unawares into "joint education," as the practice was termed at the time, but with a conscious understanding that Oberlin would be a college different from all other colleges. Above all, Oberlin founders and leaders admitted women alongside men to the college classroom because they wanted women, as well as men, to take part in the reform and regeneration of society. Oberlin, both the colony and the college, was a product of the religious evangelicalism associated with the Second Great Awakening, which called for perfecting human society as a means of bringing about God's kingdom on Earth. Women were no more exempt than men in their responsibility to bring about this great alteration, and if women could be useful in this holy work by having college educations, then they should have them. When Oberlin first offered collegiate courses in 1834, women and men took them together.[2]

Sitting in the same classroom did not mean that Oberlin made no distinction between men and women. In 1834, women were grouped in a Female Department under the control of the female principal. In their studies, they took the Ladies' Course, which did not include Hebrew,

Greek, or Latin, as did the Collegiate Course. Another way that Oberlin distinguished between men and women is that women did not read their graduation essays at commencement. But the critical difference, the separate course of study for women, was pierced in 1837, when four women applied for entrance into the Collegiate Course. The faculty admitted them, and in 1841 three of the four women became the first three female graduates of a coeducational college in the world.[3]

The roots of this Western phenomenon of collegiate coeducation may be traceable to a coeducational tradition within rural New England academies. In New England during the late 1700s, two types of female education existed. The first is much better known—urban, elite academies, the forerunners of the kinds of schools in the nineteenth century run by the likes of Emma Willard and Catharine Beecher, which emphasized gentility, making women elegant, well-mannered, and polite, glorifying their dependence upon their husbands, teaching dancing, needlework, and music, and generally, yet significantly, emphasizing the differences between men and women. The classical virtues so important to elite Americans at that time inculcated the idea that virtue was masculine, and weakness was found in femininity, with emotion rather than reason, a love of luxury rather than simplicity. Moreover, these schools looked to Europe for inspiration about the kind of education that ought to be offered.[4]

An alternative to these schools emerged in the late 1700s. In the wake of the American Revolution and ideas of republicanism, a series of coeducational academies began in New England and New York. Rural, and less concerned with gentility, the assumptions behind these schools were different from their urban counterparts. The girls who attended these schools were not being groomed for an urban life of sophistication, but for practical ends. Many of these students became schoolteachers who demonstrated the virtues of thrift and productivity. As opposed to the classical mode of thinking that emphasized differences between men and women, a Protestant ethic that presented men and women as spiritual equals gave gender differences short shrift, as did the rural and small-town environment, in which specialization was less desirable, and women and men were accustomed to working together.[5]

In addition, commercial considerations mattered, especially in New York, where founders wanted to raise property values and were not devoted to keeping girls out of the academies they founded. These commercial values ranked more highly than genteel ones over and over again. In these academies, girls and boys often sat on opposite sides of the room—not unlike many churches of the period—but their teacher was normally the same, their curriculum was often only slightly differentiated, and the education they received took place in a mixed-sex environment. The young women left school prepared to earn a living as schoolteachers and, for the young men, as ministers. They did not come from privileged backgrounds, nor did they anticipate a life of ease. Thus what they learned at school were subjects that would suit them, both female and male, for gainful employment.[6]

The tradition of coeducational academies in New England did not breach the divide between academy and college in that region. West of the Appalachian Mountains, however, and in western New York, coeducation spread into the collegiate realm. Oberlin was the only coeducational college until 1844, when Free Will Baptists opened Michigan Central College in Spring Arbor. Michigan Central was an Oberlin outpost, in essence. The founders, leaders, and faculty had strong ties to Oberlin. The first president, Daniel Graham, graduated from Oberlin, and another Oberlin graduate, Edmund Fairfield, replaced Graham in 1848. The following year the state of Michigan conferred a charter upon the college. In 1851, the school granted its first college diplomas, including a Bachelor of Science to Elizabeth D. Camp. The following year the school granted Bachelor of Science degrees to six more women and awarded its first Bachelor of Arts degree to Livonia Benedict. Soon after, the college relocated from Spring Arbor to Hillsdale and became Hillsdale College, where coeducation continued.[7]

In this instance, as in others, the Oberlin connection was close. John Shipherd, an original founder of Oberlin, went on to found coeducational Olivet College in Michigan two decades later, where he replicated his Oberlin system. Asa Mahan, a president of Oberlin during its formative years, became the first president of Adrian College in Michigan, another coeducational institution. At Alfred Academy, in western New York, an Oberlin graduate named Jonathan Allen perpetuated coeducation that already existed at the academy level when Alfred became a college.[8]

Still, other colleges without a connection to Oberlin were coeducational. Something else was going on. J. H. Fairchild would have said there was something in the soil. In 1849 the American Baptist Free Missionary Society opened New York Central College, a radical and racially integrated school in McGrawville. The following year a New York Methodist school, Genessee Wesleyan Seminary, became Genessee College, and, while it disguised the fact that women were students, was nonetheless coeducational. The spread of coeducation did not go further eastward, however, from central New York state. From 1853 onward, every year through 1860 brought more coeducational colleges, including Baldwin, Mt. Union, Antioch, Otterbein, Franklin, Urbana, Muskingum, and Heidelberg in Ohio; Earlham and North West Christian (later Butler) in Indiana; Olivet and Adrian in Michigan; Wheaton, Eureka, Monmouth, and Lombard in Illinois; Lawrence in Wisconsin; Iowa (later Grinnell), Western, and Cornell in Iowa; Alfred in western New York; and Westminster in western Pennsylvania.[9]

Gender roles in the West were less sharply distinguished than in the East. A visitor to the West from Connecticut remarked, "you cannot form any idea of difference in the young people here from those at the east all that stiffness and formality is laid aside and they are all united male and female there is no hard *feelings*, they all seem so interested in one another." Susan Rumsey Strong, in her study of collegiate coeducation at Alfred University, found that rural farm practices brought about significant overlap of male and female duties, thus creating a "rural heterogeneity" far different from the "cult of womanhood" ideology in Eastern and more urban locales, which emphasized separate spheres.[10]

The regional propensity to hand out a collegiate charter to almost any denomination fostered the birth and spread of collegiate coeducation. Many coeducational colleges founded in the 1850s were supported by small denominations with a predominantly rural, and often ethnic, laity that had a streak of sexual egalitarianism, a practical bent, and little experience with higher education. These denominations, including Free-Will Baptists, Seventh-Day Baptists, Swedenborgians, United Brethren, Society of Friends (Quakers), Disciples of Christ, Associate Reform Presbyterians, German Reform, Universalists, Associate Presbyterians, and Wesleyan Methodists, founded schools in the West, particularly in the 1850s, after the first waves of college-founding in the region.

One small denomination that sponsored a coeducational college was the New Church, or the Swedenborgians, followers of the ideas of Emanuel Swedenborg. Swedenborg, an eighteenth-century Swedish scientist, had a series of revelations late in life about biblical meaning. In and around the west central Ohio town of Urbana lived a number of New Church members, one of whom was prevailed upon to donate land to found a college. The New Church members appealed to the state government and in 1850 the Ohio legislature chartered Urbana University, which was then led primarily by Milo Williams, a Cincinnati native and New Church member. Williams insisted from the beginning that the liberal ideas of Swedenborgianism would necessitate admission of both sexes to Urbana. Thus the school began as a coeducational institution when it opened in 1853.[11]

Other coeducational colleges were sponsored by small denominations that were ethnic in character. Heidelberg College, in Tiffin, Ohio, fit this pattern. In 1850, Heidelberg was founded by Germans of the Reformed Church. These Reformed members were mostly farmers, not wealthy, and many of them still spoke German in their homes and in their worship services. From the beginning, Heidelberg offered German in its curriculum, a rarity at that time. Heidelberg was also the only Reformed Church college in the antebellum United States that was coeducational. At first women were enrolled in a "Ladies' Course" of study, but within a few years this convention was dropped, since "the ladies took the same studies the gentlemen did, and recited with them."[12]

The only two antebellum colleges to become coeducational that had been founded as male-only institutions were two small schools in eastern Ohio—Franklin College, an Associate Presbyterian school, and Muskingum College, an Associate Reformed Presbyterian institution, both of which admitted women in the late 1850s. Franklin and Muskingum were founded by Calvinistic Scotch-Irish Presbyterians, and their ethnicity was pronounced. One historian described the antebellum Associate Reformed Church in Ohio as a church that "remained as it had been founded, an immigrant church." A historian of Franklin found that during the antebellum period, a significant minority of the trustees, a majority of the faculty, and about half of the students, had Scotch-Irish names. Both of these denominations were very small. The strong abolitionist stance of the Associate Presbyterians already set them apart from most of Northern society, so they were not particularly concerned about social status and the approval of others. Two other colleges founded in the 1850s by these groups, Westminster College in western Pennsylvania (Associate Presbyterian) and Monmouth College (Associate Reformed) were coeducational from their beginnings.[13]

The United Brethren were also an ethnic church, strongly rooted among German pietists who settled in Pennsylvania and gradually moved westward. The United Brethren who founded both Otterbein University in Ohio and Western College in Iowa counted many farmers among their congregants, and they were not always the most familiar with higher education. At Otterbein, Rev. Lewis Davis, who helped found the institution and served as its president during the early years, recalled that while they were founding Otterbein, "[w]e did not just know the difference between a college and a university. We thought, somehow, that

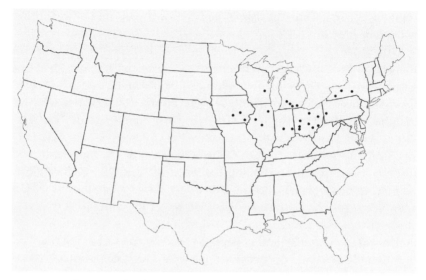

MAP 1. Coeducational colleges in the United States in 1860.

a university meant more than a college; so we took it all in and called it Otterbein University." From the beginning in 1847 until 1853 Otterbein did not even classify its students into collegiate classes or issue diplomas. The only distinction was between ladies and gentlemen, but both were admitted. Henry Garst, an Otterbein historian, wrote in 1907 that Otterbein's coeducational policies stemmed from the "genius and general spirit of the United Brethren Church," which he claimed "always accorded to women a high place, . . . a position of equality with men." United Brethren women served as "stewards, class-leaders, Sabbath-school superintendents, . . . delegates to the General Conference," and even were ordained as ministers, though not until 1889.[14]

Here we see the influence of sexual egalitarianism at work in these denominations, many of which were known for being the denominations that supported women who preached. Catherine A. Brekus found that almost all early American female preachers came from a few groups and denominations—Quakers, Freewill Baptists, Methodists, African Methodists, Millerites, and Christian Connection (including Disciples of Christ). Not surprisingly, these denominations with female preachers overlapped with those that created coeducational colleges. The denominations were not the disestablished colonial churches, but rather part of the upwelling of populistic religious fervor in the new American republic. The preaching women were generally poorer women with little education, members of denominations populated by rural members with modest means.[15]

The attitude of one Methodist appears typical. In 1843, the uncle of the president of Indiana Asbury University wrote from Cincinnati. "Last fall," he reported, "a young lady who it is said is a regularly licenced preacher in the Protestant Methodist church came by invitation to our city." He described how, during the weeks she was there, she "held protracted meetings in the reform church but preached occasionally in other places among the rest." She "was very eloquent and very impressive and did much good." She "took a good many into the reform church and they have had since that such a work as I suppose they never had before in this place." He indicated no opposition to what she was doing, and concluded, "God will work by whom he pleases."[16]

Some groups seem to have had a particularly egalitarian theological stance that placed women and men on equal footing, along with a conscious desire to go against the cultural grain. An example of this characteristic in Western coeducation is the Society of Friends, or Quakers. Because Friends believed that some part of the Divine Light resided in every person, women as well as men were encouraged to speak during the silence of their meetings for worship. The Friends were one of the least hierarchical denominations in America, and in Indiana, when the Friends Boarding School of Richmond became Earlham College in 1859, the educational mingling of boys and girls continued uninterrupted.[17]

Yet even Quakers, outside the West, did not condone coeducation. Englishman William Tallack, a visitor to Earlham College in 1860, described how "Both sexes receive the same instruction, and perform their recitations together, and also take their meals in the same large hall." Tallack noted that no other school run by the Society of Friends had such an arrangement, and that the "plan" at Earlham "is looked on with some disapproval by many of the Society eastward. But it has been found to work very well at Earlham, and has given a great stimulus to the studies of each sex, and has greatly promoted the politeness and propriety of behavior of all." The curriculum, too, satisfied Tallack, who found that their studies "both refine and strengthen their minds far more than the musical and other light accomplishments of their sisters in the eastern cities."[18]

Another example of this sexual egalitarianism would be the Freewill Baptists. Predominantly found in Maine and New Hampshire, with a peak of about 18,000 members in 1827, some Freewill Baptists moved westward into northern Ohio and southern Michigan, providing the supporters who founded Michigan Central, later Hillsdale, College in southern Michigan. Freewill Baptists were an anti-Calvinistic group. Their stout antislavery and temperance stances made them clear proponents of social reform, and the Freewill Baptists were also noteworthy for allowing and supporting female preaching. Michigan Central College and its successor, Hillsdale, were both coeducational.[19]

The exceptional denomination was the Methodist church, because it was so very large—the largest denomination in America by the 1850s. Being large, it had plenty of members who ran the gamut of financial prosperity and respectability, and could be found in both rural and urban America, in all regions of the country. The founder of Methodism, John Wesley, had encouraged women to preach, and there were Methodist women who preached in the early republic. In the Western states, as Methodists founded colleges, they varied in what they did.

Some Methodist colleges in the West became coeducational. For example, in the middle 1840s Bostonian Amos Adams Lawrence, a philanthropic Episcopalian who desired to improve morality and education in the West, offered $10,000 toward the founding of a college near lands he owned in northern Wisconsin. He acknowledged that he would most like to found an Episcopalian college, but knew that Episcopalians were few in number and not well suited to the Western region. "I have a high opinion," wrote Lawrence, "of the adaptation of the principles of the Methodists to the people of the West, and I think . . . that their institutions are carried on with more vigor, and diffuse more good with the same means, than any other." Wisconsin Methodists raised the matching $10,000 required of them and opened their preparatory department in Lawrence University in 1849, adding the first college class in 1853.[20]

The college, however, was crucially different from what Lawrence had intended. Repeatedly Lawrence wrote that he did not want the school to be coeducational. Lawrence argued that in Massachusetts, educators had raised "the standard of female education so high that physical development has been checked, and the constitution weakened. Our women," complained Lawrence, "are unhealthy and weak, and do not bear strong children; and while we are refining the intellect, we are injuring the stock." Lawrence also feared what coeducation would do to the educational level of the institution. Coeducation in other instances, believed Lawrence, had "proved highly injurious," "lowered the standard of scholarship," and "made high schools of institutions which were intended for & ought to have been colleges." Lawrence, though, was in Boston, and the Methodists in Wisconsin creating the school, who had backgrounds in coeducational settings, simply enrolled women alongside men without informing Lawrence.[21]

The two most respectable Methodist colleges, the most prosperous, really the flagship institutions of the denominations in their states, were Indiana Asbury University and Ohio Wesleyan University. Neither of these colleges admitted women, at least officially. But Samuel Wesley Williams, a student at Ohio Wesleyan in the 1840s, wrote later in life that a few girls, including Lucy Webb, who married Rutherford B. Hayes, were students. "Lucy, then in the midst of her teens, was pursuing her studies with her brothers, and, with the steward's daughter and one or two girls from the town, recited in some of the college classes, along with the young men. There was then no provision for the admission of young ladies at the college, nor did the names of the girls appear on the college catalogues. They were exceptional cases, though really students, and were thus the pioneers of that brilliant coterie of 'sweet girl-graduates.'"[22]

Some college leaders emphasized the civic and religious advantages of coeducation. In 1856, at Iowa (later Grinnell) College, nine young women who graduated from Davenport High School applied for admission to Iowa. The trustees, asked about whether the college should admit women, responded by emphasizing the "good" that could come of coeducation. As one trustee wrote of coeducation, "I should go into it with all my heart. I believe it is the way to do good. It is demanded by the spirit of the age, by the good of the rising generation, and the interests of our great state. And truly by the Cross of Christ." This emphasis was affirmed by the president of the Board, who wrote, "We must go in right away for a Female Department at Iowa College. We can do three times the good with about the same means. . . . If we don't go in for doing good the devil will get us all into the net."[23]

Other Westerners viewed the matter similarly. As one Oberlin student framed the institution in 1837, her college did not exist "to send out into the world a company of Butterflies, to glitter a while, and then vanish, but to send out a set of *pious, well-educated* and genteel (not fashionable) young Ladies prepared to be useful in any circumstances." This word, "useful," reappears again and again and captures much of the Western motivation for coeducational colleges. As Milo Williams of Urbana University put it, the learned man simply acquired knowledge and was inferior to the educated man since "[e]ducation is the developing of the powers of man, both physical and moral." The learned man "is unable to use what he has acquired; but the educated man is prepared at all times to use what he has learned. The one studies to know: the other studies to use. The one is a theorist; the other is practical. The one is comparatively useless in society; the other is prepared to do his full share in promoting the best interests of society."[24]

Generally, the West maintained a culture of usefulness. Broadly speaking, this culture consisted of two major components. The first was a largely Protestant religious impulse that called for people to reform society. The second was a mostly middle-class emphasis on practical and productive labor for the common good. The culture of usefulness rested naturally within the producer culture worldview of most nineteenth-century Americans. As opposed to the consumer culture that has dominated most of twentieth- and twenty-first-century America, in the nineteenth century a producer culture, one in which one's identity came largely from the kind of work one did, was widespread.

Westerners often used the language of usefulness. In 1832, Ohioan Hugh Smart recommended a young man to Professor Pratt, of the Granville Collegiate Institute. Smart wrote that "it is his wish to qualify him self for usefullness among us—should he appear promising I design to aid him some in geting a usefull education." A few years later Aaron Sadner Lindsley was working at a newspaper press in Illinois when he wrote a college application letter in which he explained that the year before, "at a camp meeting, I believe I gave my heart to God; and I now desire to become a useful man."[25]

Western college students of a more pecuniary mindset felt odd. John D. Hovey, after studying at Middlebury College in Vermont, moved to Ohio, where he commenced his junior year at Marietta College. Hovey wrote to a Massachusetts aunt that he was quite worried about money, which was "most dreadful scarce." Hovey had recently turned twenty-one years old and reported that he was giving thought to how he should make his way in the world. "I begin to feel some of that spirit which the people here say is so peculiar to the people of New England, that is *the money-making* spirit."[26] Hovey's letter, while certainly not the only one from a Western college student interested in money, underscores the idea that many Western college students sought their education out of a desire to become useful.

The dictates of this culture of usefulness did not release women any more than men from responsibility, and Westerners recognized colleges as places that could make one useful. In 1855, M. M. Faville wrote in the autograph book of Princess A. Miller, who studied at the Ohio Wesleyan Female College, "'We should measure our lives by usefulness, not by years.' May you prepare for usefulness by earnestly cultivating both mind and heart. Then live for some high and holy purpose and your life will be crowned, blessings ever attending you." At college, students could learn the skills necessary to succeed in business, teaching, the ministry or missionary work, or other aspects of public life. Women would not go down all of those avenues, but they could easily avail themselves of opportunities to make themselves useful.[27]

The women who attended Oberlin, whatever their course of study, exhibited their allegiance to the culture of usefulness. In 1836 forty-three female Oberlin students recorded their intentions for the future. Nine said they wanted to teach, and one added that she also wanted to "translate scriptures." Fifteen women wrote that they planned to become a "missionary," a "home missionary," or "foreign missionaries." Three others intended either to teach or become a missionary. One intended "to become qualified for instructing the ignorant," and nine expected to "prepare for whatever station the Lord directs" or enter "some sphere of Christian usefulness." These women believed that they would use their education for the enhancement of their calling, their vocation.[28]

One consideration that caused students to prefer coeducation was the opportunity to learn how to engage in debate and speak in public, cultivating their talents and making them useful. While at Oberlin, Antoinette Brown and Lucy Stone formed their own literary society with other female students, and Brown sponsored another literary society while teaching school to support her studies. Decades later, after lives of public speaking—Brown was an ordained minister, Stone a lecturer on behalf of women's rights—Stone wrote to Brown and noted that it was in their literary societies that they had "learned to stand and speak."[29]

The experiences of Brown and another Western college student, Lydia Short, indicate the changing scene. Short studied in the late 1850s at North Western Christian (later Butler) University in Indianapolis. At North Western, founded in 1855 on a coeducational basis, the men formed two literary societies, as was normal at most colleges, and admitted women as honorary members, which apparently allowed them to read prepared essays, but not to engage in rhetorical debate. One day, after listening to what she considered boring rhetoric by male members, Short and the other female students left the literary society and formed their own literary society, the "Sigournean Society." Short loved debate, which she described as "my favorite species of performance and I think it corresponds more with my tenor of mind than any other. There seems to be so much to admire, when one will boldly make an affirmation and then direct every energy to its support, or unravel the arguments of another and set forth her fallacies." These were the words of a Western woman who took a male rhetorical genre and found herself comfortable within it. When Antoinette Brown graduated from Oberlin and then returned to pursue the Theological Course, the college officials would not enroll her as a graduate student, but they allowed her to attend the classes. The Theological Literary Society, a hitherto all-male student group, included Brown as one of their number and Brown participated fully within the Society during her three years of seminary education.[30]

Another person whose life reveals the distinctive nature of coeducational collegiate life in the West is Olympia Brown, born in southern Michigan in 1835, where she was the first child of two Vermonters who had come to Michigan the previous year. As Brown related toward the end of her life, "Our chief interests outside our home while we were children lay in our outdoor excursions, in the course of which we investigated every part of our prairie and the adjacent woods, and an extensive dark and dangerous tamarack swamp." Because there was no school available, "my father built a small school house on his own land, not far from our house." Her father then canvassed the neighbors to find which ones would be willing to pay to send their children to school and board the teacher that he then procured. "Meantime, at home as well as at school, my mother was constantly pressing us forward in our studies." Years later Brown went to the nearby town of Schoolcraft for further education. "We had a 'Literary Society' in the school, of which teachers as well as pupils were members." When the teachers assigned only boys to recite and debate, and limited girls to reading, Olympia and her female friends presented a resolution to provide for equality in the literary society, only to be "suppressed" by their teachers. Outside of school, the family subscribed to the *New York Weekly Tribune*, "our only periodical literature, and indeed our oracle. Every word was read and discussed. The excellent poems printed in every issue were cut out by my mother and pasted into what she called 'verse books' for the family's reading. The radical views of the Tribune were congenial, for all members of our family were strong anti-slavery people." Brown also recalled that from Horace Greeley's newspaper she learned about "Fourierism, Woman's Rights, Dress Reform, Anti-slavery, Water-cure and all the ideas and theories then new but now either accepted and adopted or exploded and forgotten. I remember one evening in particular when they read an account of a great Woman's Rights Convention held in Worcester, Mass., October 22 and 23, 1850, two years after the first convention at Seneca Falls. Young as I was, the idea seized upon me."[31]

Brown's mother wanted Olympia to have a fine education, and Olympia tried to persuade her father to let her go to Mount Holyoke Seminary. Brown used many lines of argumentation, but found herself "tactfully dwelling upon the fact that at the Mary Lyon school we should be taught and expected to work since it was a 'manual labor school.' With her father finally convinced, Olympia Brown, her younger sister, and a friend from Schoolcraft all entered Mount Holyoke in the fall of 1854. Lyon had died years earlier, but the school was carried on by her earnest followers. "It all seemed perfect," wrote Brown, but then she discovered that the rigid rules and regimentation of the school did not suit her well. The girls' advanced studies were not recognized and they were obliged to review the basic curriculum. When Olympia and others began a literary society, their teachers sent observers to a literary society meeting, at which Olympia and her younger sister Oella debated each other, and "when the end of the term arrived the members of the Literary Society were sent for and informed that if they wished to return to the school they must understand that there would be no Literary Society. Oella Brown asked 'what is the objection; does it not make us independent?' 'Yes,' said the teacher, 'it makes you too independent.'" The Browns left Mount Holyoke after that year and turned to a school that would encourage their talents—Antioch College, in Yellow Springs, a small town in western Ohio.[32]

Some of the problem at Mount Holyoke had been theological. Brown had grown up in a place where there was no church, and she had imbibed her ideas of religion from her mother, who "cherished the teachings of the Reverend Hosea Ballou of Vermont, one of the founders of Universalism." At Mount Holyoke people placed great pressure on the Brown sisters to accept "the stern doctrines of orthodox preachers," and thus Olympia was especially pleased to join Antioch College, founded by the "Christians," and "an institution of no sectarian bias" that "imposed no doctrinal teachings upon its students."[33]

Brown loved Antioch College. When she arrived there in 1856, "I was not disappointed. Although the college was new and poor, and lacked most of the equipment thought necessary in a college even then, I found the intellectual atmosphere most congenial." Horace Mann, the president and well-known educational reformer, was a commanding influence on campus, and what impressed Brown the most, in Mann's many chapel talks, was Mann's admonition to "Be ashamed to die until you have won some victory for humanity." Brown thought Mann may have harbored some misgivings about the effects of coeducation. She wrote that he also "often exhorted us in his chapel talks to remember that we were trying 'a great experiment.' This was so frequent that it became a sort of joke with us." Mann died in 1859 without repudiating what he had helped create. Meanwhile, Brown's family, also impressed by Antioch, relocated entirely to Yellow Springs so that they could send all of their children to the college and further this "great experiment."[34]

One of the features of the college was the series of speakers who stopped there. "We had a good many lectures from such men as Horace Greeley, Wendell Phillips, Ralph Waldo Emerson and others. Every such course was arranged by students." The speakers, though, were all men, so Brown agitated for a woman lecturer. She and other students raised the money to bring Antoinette Brown. Antoinette Brown, no relation to Olympia, was the graduate of Oberlin who had done her seminary training there. At Yellow Springs she gave a lecture on Saturday evening and the next morning filled the pulpit of the Christian Church in town, where she "preached to a large audience." For Olympia it was a defining moment. "It was the first time I had heard a woman preach, and the sense of the victory lifted me up. I felt as though the Kingdom of Heaven were at hand." The success was in part the accomplishment of bringing such a notable woman to Antioch, but Antoinette Brown's presence in the pulpit was also inspiring. Olympia Brown graduated in 1860; in her autobiography she wrote, "I had already conceived the idea of studying with a view to entering the ministry."[35]

Brown applied to the Universalist divinity school at St. Lawrence University in upstate New York and began her seminary work. She supplied pulpits in the area while she studied, and in 1863, in Malone, New York, the ordaining council of the Universalists ordained Brown, whereupon she entered parish ministry. Late in life, Brown bemoaned the lack of sufficient women to spread Universalist theology. "When I read of the vain discussions of the present day about the Virgin Birth and other old dogmas which belong to the past, I feel how great the need is still of a real interest in the religion which builds up character, teaches brotherly love, and opens up to the seeker such a world of usefulness and the beauty of holiness." A long life had not dissuaded Brown from the importance of usefulness.[36]

Over the next few years, Brown pastored Universalist parishes in Vermont, Massachusetts, and Connecticut, interrupted by a few months in 1867 in Kansas, where, at the invitation of Lucy Stone, Brown worked tirelessly on behalf of women's rights legislation. The following year, 1868, back in Massachusetts, Brown felt the need for an organization exclusively devoted to woman's suffrage—all previous organizations had been mutually tied to rights for blacks and women. After talking with others, Brown "conceived the idea of this new association, secured the hall in Boston, advertised the meeting, brought the audience together, and called the meeting to order." The outcome of her efforts was the formation of the New England Woman's Suffrage Association.[37]

In 1878, she and her husband and daughter moved to Racine, Wisconsin, where she worked for the next nine years as minister to a Universalist congregation until her resignation in 1887. While Brown subsequently served various congregations on a part-time or interim basis, she put her whole energies into woman's suffrage work in Wisconsin. In 1884 she had become president of the Wisconsin Woman Suffrage Association, and she remained president until 1912. These years were filled with hard work and a lot of disappointment, but the long-lived Olympia Brown did not pass away until 1926, which meant that she was one of the few women who had been working for women's rights since the middle of the nineteenth century who lived to see full political equality with men at the ballot box in 1920.[38]

Olympia Brown, because of the span of her life, easily exemplifies the connections between the antebellum Western culture, including its colleges, and the Midwest that existed during the Progressive era. When Kathryn Kish Sklar examined the beginning of the twentieth century in Ohio, she noted that "Ohio was in many ways the best example of the American model of a relatively weak state and relatively strong civil society." Some of that strength resulted from the fact that so many women were involved in public life, which Sklar connected to the antebellum culture that fostered coeducation. "In the United States, Oberlin began the experiment in co-education during the 1830s. That experiment succeeded, and, by 1903, the culture that created co-education also found a central role for women in Ohio's reform movements." Sklar was particularly impressed by the Ohio origins in the 1870s of the Woman's Christian Temperance Union, the 208 unions (more than in any other state) in Ohio, and the WCTU's "massive direct-action tactics" that brought women down unprecedented paths of civic involvement in American life. That leadership resonated throughout the twentieth century as Midwestern women, far beyond the upbringing of Betty Friedan in Peoria, became the leaders of the modern feminist movement.[39]

Outside of the West, various obstacles impeded coeducation. The Southern educational system was designed for single-sex education, from the military academies that dotted the region, to the public universities that dominated Southern higher education and socialized young men into the Southern culture of honor. Existing scholarship shows that the college students fully understood the importance of this function of the Southern schools. At the beginning of the twentieth century, when the College of Charleston considered coeducation, students petitioned against its introduction. The students explained that letting women into the school "would inevitably tend to alter the spirit and tone of robust manliness of the student body which we believe to be of even greater importance than scholarship." During the antebellum decades, amidst the most powerful years of the culture of honor, coeducation was not an option. Furthermore, middle- and upper-class Southern white men believed that agitation for rights for women was inextricably linked to abolitionism, and consequently frowned on roles for women that lay beyond those to which women were accustomed.[40]

In New England, a long tradition of exclusively male collegiate education worked against the introduction of coeducation. Also, once again it should be noted that the established colleges had a more urban, leisured, and upper-class orientation, far different from that in the small-town, production-centered, and middle-class Western colleges. Further, many antebellum New England colleges were associated with recently disestablished churches. Overall, New England college leaders were trying to conserve their traditions rather than experiment and innovate. One sees this pattern not only in New England resistance to coeducation, but also in opposition to curricular reforms as embodied in the Yale Report of 1828, and in the hesitancy with which New England college leaders embraced reform movements of the period.

In 1846, the Society for the Promotion of Collegiate and Theological Education at the West sent two representatives, Joseph Towne and Ansel Eddy, to inspect Knox College, in Galesburg, Illinois, which had applied to the Society for financial support. The Society was skeptical of the Knox request, in part because, while women were included in the preparatory department and not in the collegiate department, the college reputedly allowed "mingling" of the sexes. Western Education Society board member Theron Baldwin acknowledged to the president of Knox College that some Western Education Society members held "strong fears with regard to the abolition & Oberlin tendencies" of Knox, and that "a union on the part of males & females as exist at Oberlin I have no doubt would be an unsuperable barrier to the reception of the Institution by our Board." Fortunately for Knox, Towne and Eddy were satisfied by their visit that Knox was not beyond the pale, and the Western Education Society voted to extend funds to Knox for a year.[41]

In New England, the eventual response to collegiate coeducation at the West was to build "sister schools," beginning with Vassar in 1865, that would complement existing all-male institutions. Over the next few decades, a number of notable schools for women appeared, joining Mt. Holyoke, which had long provided education to women. Significantly, however, almost all of these colleges did not exist until a generation, at least, and often a half century after Oberlin's doors opened to women.

Eastern and Southern opposition to coeducation increased, rather than decreased, in the late nineteenth century. Alice Hamilton, who grew up in Indiana after her birth in 1869, went to the University of Michigan in the late nineteenth century to study medicine. She pointed out that since the University had been coeducational for two decades by the time she arrived, "we women were taken for granted and there was none of the sex antagonism which I saw later in Eastern schools." Hamilton explained the habits of both politeness and egalitarianism at the University of Michigan: "A man student would step aside and let the woman pass through the door first, the women had the chairs if there were not enough to go round, but when it came to microscopes or laboratory apparatus it was first come, first served."[42]

As the example from the University of Michigan indicates, the Western trend toward coeducation continued and broadened during the middle- and late nineteenth century. Of the eight state universities to admit women by 1870, seven of the eight were Western universities. The first coeducational medical school graduates came from western New York's Geneva Medical Institute and Ohio's Cleveland Medical College. Additionally, the first fully coeducational modern research university was the University of Chicago. Founder and president William Rainey Harper hailed from small-town Ohio and graduated from Ohio's Muskingum College. Harper wanted women in every part of his university, and brought in women as undergraduates and graduate students, as faculty members and as administrators.[43]

Some Westerners were well aware that their colleges differed from Eastern schools and that Easterners did not approve of the changes. In 1837, when Oberlin founder Philo Stewart discussed Oberlin College, he pointed out that "there are many in the Eastern states who are determined that every thing at the West shall be modeled after the traditions of the fathers. But," he continued, "let us inquire what kind of institutions are needed at the West." In Stewart's sentences lies the essence of Western distinctiveness, which rested upon particular regional needs. Stewart placed local needs above tradition.[44]

Moreover, Westerners were often suspicious of New England in-fluences, which they believed were too constraining. In 1835, Eliza Dana wrote from Athens, Ohio, that a mutual acquaintance of theirs had "gone on to the East." Dana suspected that the woman would be *"yankeyfied"* there, and admitted "I have got so sick of yankies that I don't want to see one, although my ancestors sprung from that *noble race*. I boast myself in being a true blooded Buckeye. . . . I admire an independent spirit and not one that will be governed by laws made by those over-bearing yankies." Two years earlier, Mary Hovey, who had recently moved to Fountain County, Indiana, wrote to her mother that the "general opinion in New England that any thing will do for the West" was "very erroneous." Hovey said that her Indiana neighbors watched Easterners closely in the belief that Easterners tried to regu-late others' behavior. At one point, Hovey wrote, rumors spread "that I had been riding around to get subscribers to a constitution for an anti-tea & coffee society." Another rumor had Hovey traveling "round the country preaching that husbands & wives ought not to sleep together sunday nights." Hovey said that neither rumor could be further from the truth, but the anti-Eastern mentality was clearly present. Among Westerners who resisted templates of appropriate behavior imported from elsewhere, collegiate coeducation thrived.[45]

In 1883, in the *North American Review*, a writer discussing women in higher education maybe said it best when he commented that col-legiate coeducation "was an innovation that would scarcely been pos-sible, except in a new country where social prescription had no existence, where manual labor was almost a necessary adjunct to study, and where economy made it advisable. . . . It was natural that the example thus set [at Oberlin] should be followed, first in the great West, amid a popula-tion that was remarkable for its freshness and physical vigor, its passion for progress, and consequently its disregard for conventionality."[46]

Over time, of course, coeducation became the norm in American higher education and abroad. The vast majority of single-sex colleges for men and for women either opened their doors more widely to both sexes or closed altogether. These changes augured other alterations, of course, in student life and the campus climate. The next chapter delves into aspects of the lives of students, with comparisons to student life in the East and South, that show once again the distinctive regional ways of the Western colleges.

4 / Students, Piety, and Debate

Western college students differed from their counterparts in other regions. Student ages, class background, the mixture of male and female students, the emphasis on piety, the strength of the literary societies, and a lack of riots all signified a different collegiate experience in the West that highlighted a regional disposition toward civility and debate. Students, of course, were the most numerous group of people at the colleges. Just as professors sought to influence students, the students themselves had much to do with the tenor and tone of collegiate life.

Western students were older, on average, than students at Eastern and Southern colleges. When a Kenyon College student reported in 1830 that "in the college there are many between twenty and thirty years of age, and even older," he was identifying a regional trend. Prior to the Civil War at Oberlin College, for example, the average age at graduation was twenty-five; fewer than 5 percent of entering students were under the age of seventeen during the 1840s and 1850s. By way of contrast, almost half of the incoming college students at Harvard in the 1830s were under the age of seventeen; at mid-Atlantic schools such as Columbia and the University of Pennsylvania over 60 percent of entering college students were under seventeen in both the 1830s and 1850s. Even more youthful, Southern college students had the lowest average ages among students of all regions. Also, not only did Western college students tend to be older on average, but education in the West during this period was the least age-specific of any region; college students ranged from the age of about twelve to at least thirty-six years.[1]

Wealth and social background also distinguished Western college students. Age of entry often correlated to the social status of students. The young students of the South generally came from elite segments of society. Throughout the country, in most cases, the youngest college students were unable to support themselves; parents paid their way. Older college students normally taught school or took other jobs to put themselves through their course of study. In the South, this was true both at the state universities and the Southern denominational colleges. One study sampled the families of 143 students at eight Southern denominational colleges in 1850 and found that the mean family held eight times the average real estate of free white males in 1850, 90 percent of the students came from slaveholding families, and the mean number of slaves held was 24.[2]

The schools most like the Western colleges were rural New England colleges. David F. Allmendinger, Jr., found that nonelite antebellum New England colleges attracted poor farmer boys forced from the farms by declining prospects, as rocky New England soil competed poorly with large and fertile farms to the west. College administrators embraced innovation and change as they dealt with a student body different from the ones in the colonial colleges. These administrators had to provide financial help and work opportunities to students. Most students roomed and boarded with townspeople and worked as schoolteachers for three months each winter to support their education.[3]

In an essay that probed these differences among American colleges, Wilson Smith explained that in the antebellum nonurban and non-Eastern colleges he detected a vitality and sense of common purpose, fostered by the religious environment of each college. The students at these colleges, he found, came from pious Protestant families of little wealth, in contrast to the wealthy and less pious students who attended the well-established colleges.[4]

Certainly the Western college leaders tried to structure their colleges in such a way as to encourage piety among their students. While the colleges of the West were not highly sectarian during this period, religion and concerns about morality were forever present. The president of a college, as in all parts of the country, was normally a religious figure who sometimes served as a minister to a local church in addition to having his duties as president. Most professors possessed theological training and delivered sermons during all parts of the week, both on and off the college campus. In 1847, when Horace Wellington, professor of languages at Michigan Central College, wrote that he and the president of the college "preach regularly in the institution," Wellington was not describing an unusual situation, but simply relating one of the basic functions of his position. A Wabash College student found that "the President and four professors . . . appear to manifest the deepest interest in the welfare of their students, both as to moral & religious character, as well as to their intellectual development." For students throughout the region, each morning included prayer at the college chapel. In addition to literary societies, many colleges also had a Society of Inquiry, in which pious students could read religious periodicals and discuss matters of religion. College rules generally required students to attend one religious service on Sunday; most students could easily attend two or three.[5]

Regular religious revivals punctuated this continuous exposure to religion. The president of Ohio Wesleyan wrote in 1850 that the college, founded in the 1840s, had "enjoyed a revival every year." College leaders considered revivals a part of the institutional mission and the educational experience. A father of an Ohio Wesleyan student wrote to his friend in February 1847 that a revival had been ongoing in Delaware, Ohio, for two weeks, that many students had "been converted," and that "the religious feeling at the University is so great & so general, that the college studies had to be suspended, sometimes." Educators would halt the usual coursework for days or even weeks to allow the revival full sway over students' lives.[6]

Students pleased with their education thanked former professors for attention to their spiritual well-being. Benjamin Harrison, later president of the United States, attended Farmers' College in Ohio before he transferred to nearby Miami University. After the transfer, Harrison extended to Robert Hamilton Bishop, a Farmers' professor, "my warmest thanks for the lively interest you have ever manifested in my welfare and advancement in religious as well as scientific knowledge." A few years later, in another letter to Bishop, Harrison "gratefully remembered" the "kind interviews which you repeatedly gave me on the subject of my soul's future interests." Professors not only worked with students in the classroom, helping them to pursue their academic studies; professors also assisted students with their spiritual welfare.[7]

Students sometimes came to Western colleges because of this emphasis on moral education. A University of Vermont sophomore who desired to transfer to Oberlin explained in 1836 that he was leaving the University of Vermont because "while the officers of the University are diligent and unsparing in their efforts to thoroughly discipline the intellectual powers, they woefully neglect the *moral training* of their students." Likewise, a Middlebury College student who desired to transfer to Oberlin the following year expressed similar sentiments when he justified the move because the "subject of *religion* is *greatly neglected* here. The *cultivation* of *piety* and *holiness*," he found, was "the last thing thought of." Tutors, professors, and students of Middlebury all concurred "that as a general thing, students come out of college with less religion or piety than they had when they went in." In 1841, Reverend J. Mills of Washington, Pennsylvania, wrote to Matthew Simpson, president of Indiana Asbury. Mills reported that he was dissatisfied with the collegiate education his son was receiving in Washington, Pennsylvania, because of the "unwarrantable laxity in reference to the students . . . & such a thing as the conversion of one to *God*, is unheard of at any time." Mills considered sending his son to study under Simpson "or some other person similarly situated, who will feel some *concern*, not only for his literary, but his moral & Religious training."[8]

Western college students never complained similarly. If anything, they protested that the moral and religious influences of the college were too strong. Rutherford B. Hayes, another future president, was among only ten students not "changed" when a revival swept through Kenyon College in 1839. Hayes pointed to the divide between students influenced and not influenced by the revival when he bemoaned the fact that because of the revival, "[e]very single one of my best friends are 'gone,' as it is called." Other students greeted revivals with cynicism. A. B. Morse studied at Agricultural College in Lansing, Michigan, where he received a letter from a former student, Caleb Manchester. Manchester asked Morse, "Did they get up a general revival . . . and try to convert all of the so called sinners to come and kneel at the throne of grace and make long prayers? How sick I did get at all of this professional religion when I was there."[9] Undeterred by such critics, Western college leaders never doubted that religious faith and academic inquiry inhabited the same realm.

Another part of the structure of college student lives was the literary society. The literary society first appeared in colonial New England colleges and then spread throughout collegiate education. After the mid-nineteenth century, the literary society went into decline in all regions except for the West, as fraternities and other secret societies competed for the social activities of the students and as colleges absorbed many of the educational functions of the literary societies into the standard curriculum. The unique vitality of the literary societies in the West allowed them to prosper alongside fraternities and changing curricula into the twentieth century.[10]

During the antebellum period in the Western colleges, the literary society was a pivotal institution in the lives of many students. Normally, almost every college student belonged to a literary society and each college had two competing societies, each with a library of books and periodicals. The literary society membership met weekly to debate questions or resolutions, read essays and poetry, and critique each other. Though the literary society functioned under the auspices of the college leadership, faculty members did not participate in the meetings. Rather, the literary society functioned because of student initiative, which encouraged student independence and leadership, as students learned how to create and shape the social structures in which they participated.

Despite the fact that proceedings of the society were secret, students were hardly locked away in their literary society meeting rooms. Society members sometimes invited guests to view their proceedings. Also, though the literary societies met separately during the school term, at the end of the term they engaged each other in public competition, sending forth their best to orate and debate, often in front of a large audience. An Indiana University senior in 1846 attended an exhibition at Indiana Asbury. He wrote in a letter, "I went to *Greencastle* last week to see the '*animals*' of that college show off . . . And a greater string of bombast I never heard (or saw) spun—All of our class went." Parents and townspeople, along with students from other colleges, attended these public affairs. An English observer of antebellum American colleges was astonished by the large number of public speaking exercises that went on in these schools compared to institutions of higher education in England. The Americans loved to declaim—colleges were a special training ground for that practice.[11]

The first year of operation of one literary society illustrates the values and the range of activities embraced by college students. At Granville College in Ohio, a literary society, the Calliopean, formed in 1835. The charter members quickly wrote a constitution and by-laws, elected officers, and decided to meet weekly. The Calliopean Society was clearly connected to Granville College itself. If a member were expelled from the College, he would also be expelled from the Society. All Society activities, including changing the constitution or by-laws, had to be approved by the faculty.[12]

Almost as soon as they formed, the members authorized the purchase of a bookcase and sent a detail to Columbus with instructions also to purchase the Harper's Family Library. The students did so, finding a seventy-two volume set, which they shelved in the bookcase. This collection constituted the beginning of the Society's library and also demonstrated the academic values that underlay the Society.[13]

The membership increased quickly when the Calliopeans elected sixty-one honorary members in April and two months later elected forty-eight more. Through an examination of the list of honorary members one gains clues about the aspirations of the students and about their models of behavior. Some honorary members were the most notable living national political figures, including John Quincy Adams, Andrew Jackson, Martin Van Buren, John C. Calhoun, Daniel Webster, and Henry Clay. The Calliopeans also elected authors such as James Fenimore Cooper, and important Ohioans, including political figures such as William Allen and William Henry Harrison; Daniel Drake, a doctor, writer, and early state leader; and Caleb Atwater, politician and author of the first history of Ohio.[14]

The intentions of the Society in electing honorary members were twofold: first, they hoped honorary members would contribute funds or books to the support of the Society; second, by electing honorary members and opening correspondence with them, the students hoped to establish connections to a public world of politicians, lawyers, ministers, educators, and authors. If an honorary member responded to the notice of his membership by thanking the society or by sending a volume from his personal library, this event was potentially the beginning of an association the students could use to their advantage. The corresponding secretary of each society had a most coveted job, which allowed one to correspond with men of distinction around the country.[15]

That same April, the Calliopeans established "a Historical and Philosophical Department" of the Society, "designed for collecting and preserving all such facts relating to the civil and natural history of the Western country, especially of the early settlements, as may be deemed worthy of preservation." Part of the reason for establishing this department was that the members wanted to fill "a *Cabinet of Curiosities*" with "Natural, Mineral, and Artificial Specimens—such as rocks, minerals, petrifactions, shells, Indian Antiquities, and other objects of curiosity." Beyond the curricular offerings, the literary society provided an outlet for other academic pursuits, such as scientific and historical interests.[16]

The next month the society members met to determine whether to expel one of their number. The Calliopeans tried Lewis Granger on the charge that "he encouraged and was engaged in a mob against a portion of his fellow students and a lawful meeting of citizens." As J. H. Fetters, a Calliopean, testified to the assembled, he had attended a meeting held at the schoolhouse. There, "Mr. Alvord lectured on Abolitionism—toward the close of the meeting a disorderly mob made its appearance and broke up the assembly, by throwing stones & eggs into the windows—The students present & some others pursued the intruders" and Fetters had seen Granger run away. Others testified as well; apparently Granger had not only been part of the mob, but an instigator. Granger was removed from the Society by a vote of nineteen to one.[17]

Significantly, the Calliopeans booted Granger for inciting a mob against a lawful gathering, rather than for his political views. The breach of rights of assembly and expression of ideas, the enlistment of violence to suppress opinion, was Granger's egregious failing. The Calliopeans were unafraid of ideas, willing to allow those in opposition to have their say. The rule of mobs was anathema; the ability of citizens to gather lawfully must be protected.

Special occasions gave students chances to foster unity within their societies. On July 4, 1836, the Calliopean members met early in the morning at the Baptist Meeting House and then proceeded in a carriage to an impressive set of Indian mounds near Newark, which they intended to excavate in hopes of finding items to add to their Cabinet of Curiosities. Upon their arrival, "the company were drawn up in a line, and gave three hearty cheers in honor of the day and occasion. After which the Declaration of Independence was read." They set to digging and found skeletons, arrowheads, and other items.[18]

The capstone of the year came the following month, August, when they celebrated the first anniversary of the Calliopean Society. William Allen of Chillicothe, one of the honorary members of the Society, gave an address, which the Society then had printed and, after purchasing one thousand copies, sent to honorary members and other literary societies. Having a notable public figure address a literary society was standard, as was printing the address at society expense for distribution to all who might be interested. The practice represented a desire to hear the words of important individuals and to make connections between the college students and invited speakers.[19]

In that first year, through orations and debates, through exploratory outings and internal discipline, the Calliopean Society members prepared for entry into a public world beyond the college. They proved their allegiance to a particular vision of civil discourse and interaction. In many respects, the literary society functioned as a collegiate training ground for participation in public affairs. Literary society proceedings from college to college are standard in their descriptions of debates and orations. Existing essay books show that essays were normally quite conventional, often on topics such as "Our Country's Prospects," or "Personal Responsibility." Students debated questions such as "Should slavery be abolished?" or "Are mental resources and moral energy most developed in worldly men?" Many members found the literary society exercises enjoyable, though rarely profound. Yet, despite the ordinary nature of much that transpired, these organizations were highly significant because of their role of instilling habits of serious inquiry, thought, writing, and open debate. Weekly, surrounded by books and curiosities, the members practiced the habits of democratic and engaged wrestling with ideas.

In the 1850s, what had been national took on more regional form. It is true that the literary societies existed nationally, even if in Southern colleges ideas about honor pervaded the literary societies, making them arenas in which Southern college men jockeyed, sometimes violently, for power and respect. But in the 1850s the rise of fraternities, especially in the Northeast, sounded the death knell for literary societies in that region. The same was true in the South, which also gravitated toward fraternal organizations. Fraternities made inroads in the Western states, though some schools forbade them. Yet the literary societies maintained their strength into the twentieth century. It may be that what made the Western literary societies so strong and so popular, giving them longevity and meaning long after their purpose had been lost elsewhere, was a regional disposition toward debate.

Daniel Drake argued that because Westerners lacked newspapers during the early years of settlement, citizens substituted debate for the printed word. The practice continued, on its own merits, long after the West filled with newspapers. The tendency to debate was strong in the West. College students were hardly the only individuals who debated. John Calvin Hanna recalled in his autobiography that, while a youth in southern Illinois during the 1820s, "Two or three winters we had a debating society in the neighborhood which I attended pretty regularly and there laid the foundation of my success in debates afterwards." Recalling that debate society brought to Hanna's mind "the existence of a similar society when I was but nine years old. . . . I was never present at a meeting of that society except once when it was held at my father's house." At the age of seventeen, Hanna told his father he wanted to go to college. Hanna went to Hanover College in Indiana for only a brief time. In 1841, however, at the age of twenty-five, married with a child, and teaching school for a living, Hanna "decided to again try to go to college.

I got a teaching position near Hanover and attended the meetings of the Philadelphian Society and participated in the debates and was greatly benefitted by the exercises."[20] For Hanna, the debates in his early years were significant, formative events.

Public debates, some better known than others, some lasting days, were a feature of Western society. Frequently publishers would hire someone to transcribe what was said and then print the proceedings for purchase. Other debate appears to have been more informal. During the 1850s, schoolteacher John M. Roberts normally engaged in planned, weekly debates during the winter months at area schoolhouses, though he was open to impromptu debates, as when he tangled with some Catholics one evening over whether priests were infallible.[21]

Most people were apparently quite willing to engage in debate. One rare example of resistance to an outright invitation to debate comes from a New Englander in the West, a representative of the American Home Missionary Society, who, in 1832, wrote from Indiana that the "*Campbellites* . . . used every exertion to draw us into a controversy with them, but I declined." The consternation of this missionary, who worked for an organization with close ties to a newly disestablished church in New England, demonstrates how the situation in much of New England was not predicated on the opportunity for open debate about doctrinal matters. In the West, in some instances, preachers finished speaking and then offered their pulpit to anyone who wanted to disagree. No single denomination held such an advantage over rival groups that religious partisans need not defend their beliefs publicly.[22]

The literary society debates within the colleges did not preclude debates nearby. W. B. Riggin, at McKendree College in Lebanon, Illinois, wrote in 1844 that besides college debates, "The debate in town is still continued; They meet every once in a while." In 1837, a recently arrived professor of classics at Miami University wrote that abolition "has not been publickly discussed since I came, at the Institution; yet there have been several debates, in the neighborhood adjacent to Town." College students who taught school also witnessed and encouraged debate. Abraham Bartholomew, teaching at a new Lutheran seminary in Columbus, Ohio, wrote in 1841 that "The number of students has now increased to 17. . . . Seeing, therefore that this institution bids fair to become one of the most eminent in our state, I have endeavoured to form a debating society." In one of the most memorable accounts of Western debate, in 1850 Elijah Edwards, a student at Indiana Asbury, taught at a school in Romney, in Tippecanoe County. Edwards found that the residents of

Romney were no strangers to debate. One evening the Romneyites invited the Canadians, who lived across the river, to debate at the school-house. Edwards recorded in his diary that the "momentous question was thus stated—'Resolved:—*That a dog is more serviceable than a gun.*' The Canadians . . . contended hotly for the dogs, while the romeyites stubbornly stood up for the guns." The argument was both long and heated, and Edwards concluded that "Fortunately there were neither dogs nor guns present, or the contest might [have] ended disastrously with roar of gun and yalp of cur."[23]

This love of debate, however, became crowded out in other regions. During the middle of the nineteenth century, the rise of fraternities signaled the end of most collegiate literary societies in the East and South. While fraternities advanced in popularity, in the Southern states secret societies were also popular within higher education. A prominent model for student secret societies was the Masons, who were heavily involved in Southern higher learning, and sometimes founded and controlled schools. At many Southern colleges Masons played an important role in placing the cornerstone of campus buildings.[24]

The Southern student experience was also shaped, in part, by the system of slavery. It helped to structure student expectations and behavior. Southern students arrived at college with more than books; often they brought slaves with them. The history of the University of Mississippi records that the student leader of the campus military company was not the only student to "come up to college with two horses, a body-servant, hunting dogs, and guns." At the University of Alabama, Oran Roberts arrived in 1833 with a slave, Prince, whose labor he sold in the town to help pay his college expenses. Only slightly more modestly, John William Burgess recalled that in 1861 he started from home for Cumberland University, in Tennessee, "with a trunk of clothing, a box of books, a box of tallow candles, and a Negro boy. . . . a lumbering family coach, drawn by two stout horses, and guided by a Negro driver, conveyed me and my boy, together with all my other paraphernalia, to my destination."[25] For wealthy students, being waited on at college by slaves, whether their own or those who belonged to the college, was not unusual. At the University of North Carolina, the slaves who cleaned the dormitory and recitation rooms also, for a fee, blacked student boots or toted packages for them. Most Southern colleges were built, in part, by slave labor, and colleges routinely hired or owned slaves. As one Southern observer summed up Southern education: "A southern man is educated in nine cases out of ten to be a gentleman, a term which sometimes means a hapless being who is dependent on others for even the smallest offices of labor."[26]

Southern college students frequently accosted slaves. At the University of Georgia, students were admonished for chasing the slaves. At the University of Alabama, one student recalled, when the biscuits were not light enough, a biscuit "might be seen flying toward a negro-waiter, which would be succeeded by a whole volley of them from all parts of the hall, until every waiter had fled through the back-door." Other instances were more serious: at the University of Alabama, students beat slaves, one of whom required surgery to treat his wounds. In another incident, a slave named Moses, who had been stabbed by a student with a table-fork the year prior, had his right arm injured when a student swung a crutch at him. Students branded slaves at the University of Mississippi.[27]

Other times, students used slaves and perhaps free blacks as sexual partners. In some instances, students visited brothels; other times, they took advantage of slaves belonging to presidents and professors. Basil Manly, president of the University of Alabama, wrote of "Morgan," a slave belonging to Professor Barnard, "This boy, Morgan, acts as Pimp to get out Barnard's women—especially the younger Luna; whom [the students] use in great numbers, nightly." Violence and degradation sometimes went hand in hand. At the University of North Carolina, William Sydney Mullins recorded in his diary that one night in 1840 a group of students "blacked themselves, went down to a negro house[,] seized Suky Maysh, a common negro prostitute, tore off her clothes, and painted her naked body!!!" The most public of these instances came in 1859 at the University of Mississippi, where two students went into the chancellor's home while the chancellor and his wife were out of town. A subsequent faculty investigation concluded that the two students had intruded with "shameful designs" on one of the "defenseless female servants," Jane. Jane evidently resisted, and was "cruelly outraged and beaten" so badly by one of the students that she could not work for days; her bruises remained visible for two months.[28]

When students from this culture entered institutions in free states, the cultural differences were evident. Ralph Waldo Emerson remarked in 1837, "The young Southerner comes here a spoiled child, with graceful manners, excellent self-command, very good to be spoiled more, but good for nothing else,—a mere parader. He has conversed so much with rifles, horses and dogs that he has become himself a rifle, a horse and a dog, and in civil, educated company, where anything human is going forward, he is dumb and unhappy."[29]

Emerson's stereotyping apparently had some basis in fact, as testified by the letter of application one slave-state applicant, Riddelle, wrote to

Earlham College, the Quaker school in Indiana, in the 1850s to apply for admission for himself and his younger brother. They requested a catalogue and explained that

> We would like to bring a servant and our guns and dogs to hunt on holidays. We are from St. Louis and have been in Bloomington [at Indiana University] seeing the college here. The inhabitants here are not as aristocratic as I would wish them to be and therefore I do not like them. I suppose if we pay a higher price we can obtain a separate table. Our servant will take care of it. It will not make much difference as to what kind of room you give my servant but I would like to have a nicely furnished room as near my Brother's as possible. If you have stables near the college I would like to bring my horse, my Brother his pony. We have been at Yale for the last year but not liking the place we had returned when we heard of the University at Bloomington.[30]

Riddelle and his brother evidently had little acquaintance with Quakers. In any case, they never became students at Earlham.

Typically, historians have focused on the propensity of antebellum college students to riot, depicting the antebellum years as "a period when constant warfare raged between faculty and students.... It was preeminently a period of rowdies, riots, and rebellions." Or historians have characterized this period as a time when "[a]ll over the new nation colleges experienced a wave of collective student uprisings." In 1840, for example, at the University of North Carolina, drunken students tore down the professors' stables and rode the professors' horses through town, broke the windows of tutors' rooms, and stoned members of the faculty. The same year, University of Virginia students shot and killed Professor John A. G. Davis as he attempted to stop a group of rioting students. Other student riots, dozens, took place at schools such as Harvard, Yale, Geneva (New York), Princeton, Randolph-Macon (Virginia), Davidson (North Carolina), University of Georgia, and University of Mississippi. During these riots students discharged firearms, threw rocks, brawled with townspeople, and generally damaged property, especially college classrooms and buildings.[31]

Careful observers have pointed out that state university students in the South were more violent than their denominational college counterparts. Students in non-Eastern and nonurban colleges were least likely to riot. No riots whatsoever took place in the West, as far as I can discover. No other scholar of antebellum college riots has discovered riots in Western colleges. Unhappy Western students resolved their dissatisfaction with college leaders in other ways. These students negotiated collectively with college leaders and rejected violence in favor of other means, including strikes and even mass withdrawal. In the region with a distinctive student body—older and not single-sex, more pious and lacking an elite background, and given to civil debate—the students acted differently from students in other regions; they pursued alternatives to violence.

J. J. Hopkins, a Hillsdale College graduate who reminisced about his antebellum college years, remembered that on one occasion the president of the college found students decorating the chapel for commencement and sent the students to their rooms because they did not have permission. "Then was there a rebellion indeed!" The students abandoned their recitations and held mass meetings instead. They formed committees and petitioned "for a redress of grievances." The students met with faculty members and made "inflammatory speeches and threats . . . that the college would be abandoned unless the decree was recalled." In the end, though, Hopkins concluded, "everything went on as before." The matter blew over.[32] Hopkins's tale matters because he reported that not only did the students fail to resort to violence, but he told what they did do: abandon classes, meet with other students, form committees, petition leaders, make speeches, and threaten withdrawal. These behaviors would be repeated elsewhere in the West.

One significant example comes from the well-known story of Lane Seminary in 1834 and 1835. In 1834 the students of Lane Seminary determined to debate the subject of slavery, colonization, and abolitionism. Most faculty members were less than thrilled, as Lane stood only two miles from Cincinnati, a city tied strongly to the slave-holding South, and a city not known for abolitionism or other critiques of slavery. Undeterred, the students ignored faculty concerns and debated their questions two and a half hours each day for eighteen days.[33]

By the end of the debate in March, almost every student had become convinced of the evils of slavery and the need for slavery's immediate end, so students formed the Lane Anti-Slavery Society in connection with the American Anti-Slavery Society. Equally important, the students acted upon their convictions and took their antislavery message to Cincinnati whenever possible. Students began working among the African Americans of Cincinnati, speaking to them at lecture halls, setting up a circulating library and reading room, and teaching reading schools, Sabbath schools, and Bible classes in the African-American community.

Two students took leaves of absence from Lane in order to teach full-time, while other students began to disseminate antislavery propaganda.[34]

Most Cincinnati citizens responded negatively to these changes. Formally, critics published letters in newspapers and magazines that chastened the students for being swept up by current events and neglecting their studies. Informally, the students and everyone else associated with Lane Seminary received threats of violence against the seminarians, the seminary, and abolitionism in general. For the trustees of Lane, most of whom were established Cincinnati businessmen, respected Presbyterians, and anti-abolitionists, the situation was quite uncomfortable. As a result, while most students were away during the summer break between terms, the trustees met to discuss the matter. In early October, with the school set to begin on the fifteenth of October, the college leaders made their decision. They voted to ban all student organizations lacking faculty approval and forbade students from meeting together, making speeches, or leaving Lane Seminary grounds without faculty approval. They specifically ordered the student antislavery and colonization societies to disband and they reasserted their authority to dismiss students from Lane at any time.[35]

Upon returning, students learned of the new rules. In response, the students asked the faculty for an explanation of the rules, which the faculty provided. Students then asked permission to discuss the new regulations among themselves. The faculty denied this request, and when the students asked permission to discuss among themselves whether or not to stay at Lane, permission was again denied. Faced with this situation, thirty-nine of the forty-six returning students withdrew, and eight of the seventeen students who were newly arrived refused to enroll. Turnover continued until by the end of the school year seventy-five students had left Lane, fifty-one of whom said they did so because of the actions of the faculty and trustees. It was a devastating year for Lane.[36]

About a dozen students remained together in the town of Cumminsville, near Cincinnati, where they attempted to continue their Cincinnati work and their studies. After a few months in Cumminsville they met with John J. Shipherd of Oberlin College. At the time, Oberlin was a new and small college that struggled in the shadow of nearby Western Reserve College. Shipherd was a founder of Oberlin who, when he learned what had happened at Lane Seminary, went to Cumminsville and invited the former Lane students to come to Oberlin. The students agreed to Shipherd's request, but not unconditionally. The students wanted Asa Mahan, a Lane trustee who was sympathetic to the students, to become the president of Oberlin. The students asked that John Morgan, a Lane professor who had supported their debates and whom the trustees subsequently fired, become a professor at Oberlin. Further, they wanted Oberlin to guarantee all students freedom of speech and allow admission to Oberlin with no consideration of race. Oberlin trustees were leery of some of the conditions, but the prospect of enrolling the Cumminsville students and perhaps other Lane students was too much to turn down. Oberlin leaders met the students' requests; ultimately thirty-two of the Lane Rebels studied at Oberlin, helping to transform a cipher of a college into one of the most significant schools in the United States.[37]

The Western ways were on display again in 1840, when Granville College students loudly celebrated Independence Day after their classes ended on July 3, in the same building where a recitation continued. The professor went upstairs and asked a student, Miller Moody, who was making so much noise. Moody said nothing, the noise suddenly stopped, and the professor returned to his classroom. A few days later students were surprised when the faculty dismissed the student, Moody, from the college.[38]

Students concerned about the dismissal held a meeting, which resulted in a delegation that visited the acting college head, Professor Stevens, to ascertain exactly why Moody had been dismissed. Stevens informed the committee that Moody had been sent away because he would not agree to provide information about his classmates when so directed by college authorities. Most of the students, indignant, signed a protest in which they approved of what Moody had done and avowed they would do likewise in similar circumstances. They delivered their response to Stevens, who did not immediately respond, but on the final day of the term Stevens asked to meet with all of the students who had signed the protest. At the meeting, Stevens defended the faculty, criticized the students, and announced that he expected all of the students who had signed the protest to sign a request that their signatures be withdrawn from the document. The students refused to sign and immediately left for vacation following commencement exercises. Ultimately, however, Stevens had his way, as he required students who returned the following term to remove their name from the protest as a condition of their admittance. The students apparently complied.[39]

In 1856, at Muskingum College in New Concord, Ohio, a student named Francis H. Herdman wrote an impertinent letter to a professor with whom he was dissatisfied. The professor complained to the trustees, who suspended Herdman for the three weeks remaining in the term. The next morning, though, when Herdman's punishment began, twenty-six of Herdman's fellow Union Literary Society members left the college, along with many of the other literary society's members. As one student recalled, the students "took their ease and walked the streets as independent as retired merchants." For Muskingum, which had only within the previous decade risen above the academy level to establish a regular collegiate course of study, the incident was alarming. Trustees examined the president and two professors on the matter and heard petitions from townspeople of New Concord, who were interested in Muskingum College as an important local institution. Eventually most students returned; the professor the students had criticized left the college.[40]

A final notable example of nonviolent conflict between students and faculty at a Western college comes from the same year, 1856, at Indiana Asbury University. There, students normally met in their literary societies for debates and orations each Friday evening. But during the 1855–1856 school year the college president and faculty discussed moving the meeting time of the literary societies to the afternoon, because the societies were meeting until late in the evening, oftentimes to 10:30 and sometimes almost until midnight. Further, the faculty suspected that both during and after the meetings some society members were risking their moral health. At the close of the 1855–1856 year, the president and faculty decided that in the coming school year the literary societies would meet during the afternoon.[41]

When Indiana Asbury reopened, though, the professors were busy with other things and did not immediately insist on the Friday afternoon meeting time. The societies met on Friday evenings for weeks until, on October 17, President Daniel Curry sent a letter to each literary society that instructed the societies to meet on Friday afternoons between two and six o'clock. The students objected and formed committees to meet with the faculty to raise objections and plead their case. The faculty did not relent, at which point the students met and decided that if they could not have evening meetings then they would suspend the literary societies altogether.[42]

This was a bold move on the students' part, since the literary societies were a crucial component of the collegiate education. Moreover, scores of students met outside of town on Saturday, October 25, to discuss the situation. This action appears to have alarmed the college leaders greatly, as the following Monday President Curry spoke to the students publicly about what was happening. The faculty claimed that Curry "earnestly admonished the young men to cease their agitations, assuring them that if they did so the matter should stop at this point, and no further inquiry be made." The students said that, indeed, Curry had told the students to stop agitating, and "at the same time *threatened* them . . . that if any more meetings were held, or other demonstrations of dissatisfaction were shown, he would 'expel' every such offender from the institution."[43]

Curry was running into problems that may have reflected his lack of experience. In 1854 the faculty experienced wholesale turnover when the president and three other prominent faculty members resigned. Curry had not been a college leader previously and did not become president of Indiana Asbury until late in 1854, and thus Curry and his faculty had governed the school for less than two years.[44]

The next day, Tuesday, the faculty and students agreed to meet amicably and settle their dispute. After the faculty spoke and explained their reasoning, they yielded to W. F. Stone, a senior student, who told the faculty that the students saw their meeting time as a "right" not subject to faculty interference, and intimated that the students were willing to leave the school altogether rather than give up that right. Curry dismissed the meeting at this point, and the matter escalated further. The following day, at chapel, Curry presented the students with an ultimatum that, if rejected, would result in suspension from the college. Acceptance would absolve the student of all responsibility for his actions to that point. Each student had twenty-four hours in which to consider his response, and the roll would be called at prayers the next day, at which each student had to answer "yes" or "no" when asked whether he would sign the document.[45]

The ultimatum itself was a pledge:

I promise in all things, as a Student and a member of Indiana Asbury University, that, so long as I sustain that relation, I will be subject to its laws, and to the regulations and discipline of the Institution.

I entirely disclaim for myself as a Student, and for any and all association of Students any rights or privileges, not secured by said laws and discipline.

I further promise that I will abstain from all words and actions of every kind, in opposition to the government of the Institution; and that I will not do anything, directly or indirectly to render any fellow-student dissatisfied with the government of the institution, or to induce any one to leave it.

While the president and faculty apparently thought this a reasonable document, in the students' minds, the pledge brought an entirely new issue into the conflict. Almost every student would willingly agree to the first part, but most students believed that the second and third portions were not corollaries of the first. Moreover, students objected to the last section as a denial of their rights of free speech. The following day, of the approximately eighty-eight students who answered, sixty-nine, including all twenty-two members of the senior class, refused to accept. The faculty suspended every one of the refusers.[46]

The college continued to function, since, besides the college-level students, over one hundred other students uninvolved in the dispute were enrolled in preparatory and normal work. But the suspension of the larger portion of the collegiate classes was a serious event and brought townspeople into the conflict. The local newspaper, the *Putnam Republican Banner*, criticized the president and faculty for lacking restraint and tact. The public could hardly ignore the suspended students, "now out on furlough," the newspaper reported, "loafing about town."[47]

In light of these unusual events, the trustees called a special meeting and convened on December 16 to investigate the state of affairs. After hearing from the college leaders, the trustees issued a statement in which they ostensibly stood by the faculty, but they also said clearly that they wished the affair had been handled differently, they ended the suspension of all students, and the trustees invited all students to return. No mention was made of the literary society meeting times, but they soon resumed their meetings on Friday evenings. Some suspended students returned to Indiana Asbury, but not one of the seniors did. Indiana Asbury had lost the entire senior class. Many of the withdrawn seniors went to other schools, especially Indiana University, from which nine of the twenty-two graduated the following spring. At the same time, when the school year ended, Daniel Curry resigned his presidency.[48]

The experience at Indiana Asbury contained similarities to what had happened at Hillsdale, Lane, Granville, and Muskingum. Repeatedly, Western students acted in response to their grievances, yet they also exercised their agency in nonviolent ways and remained within the bounds of respectable behavior. In comparison with other regions, Western college students behaved differently from Southerners and from students at elite Eastern schools. The structure of the colleges, in combination with the backgrounds of the students, made the Western collegiate experience distinctive, and throws the particularity of the West into greater relief.

Even as these students pursued their studies, many of them were also engaged with a broader community. As they graduated, by the hundreds and eventually thousands, they spread out through the region, carrying the values of the colleges with them. The following chapter shows that the Western colleges were integrated into the region. The lives of some Western college graduates demonstrate the direct influence of the colleges in a later period, the Progressive era. And the chapter demonstrates that the values of the antebellum Western colleges, consonant with the regional culture of the West, yielded a regional disposition toward invention and scientific inquiry.

5 / From West to Midwest

This chapter focuses on a striking trait of the (Middle) Western colleges during the late nineteenth and early twentieth centuries—their propensity for the production of scientists. For over a half century, the colleges with the highest percentages of graduates who became scientists were clustered in the Middle West. This trait was connected to the characteristics of the antebellum Western colleges, and signifies a key continuity in the strand of Midwestern culture to which the colleges contributed, and of which they were so much a part.

The manual labor programs of the early nineteenth century proved amenable to scientific agricultural study, and more generally, to academic study that involved contact with the physical world. The egalitarianism embedded in manual labor programs found a natural outlet in late nineteenth-century Baconian scientific inquiry, in which observation—democratically available to all—was the basis of scientific investigation and discovery, at a time when expensive laboratories were not necessary. Also, in the nineteenth century some people regarded the natural sciences as inherently a female discipline, as opposed to the masculinity of classical studies. The same Western cultural milieu that fostered coeducation by breaking down gender divisions in learning cultivated scientific inquiry by including scientific study in the standard curriculum. And the middling-class, rural, and small-town origins of Western college students, combined with their pietistic Protestant backgrounds, caused them to look upon science as a respectable path to a higher socioeconomic status, as well as to a vocation that would benefit society.

This chapter, far more speculative than exhaustive, begins with the stories of two antebellum Western college students—John Wesley Powell and Harvey W. Wiley—and follows their paths to scientific exploration and investigation as life-long passions and careers. Wiley, as a key figure in the Progressive era because of his association with the creation of the Food and Drug Administration, opens a brief discussion of the relationship of the Progressive era to the Midwest as a region. Historian Robert Crunden saw the Progressive era, with its great respect for science and invention, as having been birthed in the Midwest, and showed that the Progressive leaders came disproportionately from the Midwest, especially from its denominational colleges, after growing up in pietistic homes. The father of Wilbur and Orville Wright, the Reverend Milton Wright, illustrates this point. The chapter then analyzes the study that showed the pronounced tendency of Midwestern college graduates to become scientists, and discusses how Robert Noyce, as well as his contemporaries and predecessors in his field of study, connected closely to the traditions of the antebellum Western colleges.

The chapter concludes with the observations of two antebellum Westerners, Daniel Drake and Andrew Wylie, on the particularities of their region. Drake and Wylie were boosters, to be sure, but notwithstanding their sometimes overblown rhetoric they pointed to ideals that many Westerners actualized over time as they created a regional culture in America, one with implications that still resound, both within and without the Midwest.

* * *

John Wesley Powell exemplifies the relationship of these Western colleges to scientific investigation. Born in 1834 in western New York to Welsh Methodist parents who had immigrated to the United States in 1830, as a boy "Wes" Powell moved with his parents to southern Ohio. Jackson County, their place of residence, was home to numerous Welsh settlers. Wes's father, Joseph, preached to various congregations in the vicinity and beyond the county, and he supported his family through a tailor business and some speculation in land lots. Whether he was home or away, Joseph's wife Mary, a follower of Swedenborgian principles, gathered the large family together at the beginning and end of each day for prayer, religious song, and Bible reading. Wes recalled, later in life, that as a boy he memorized all four gospels from the King James Bible.[1]

Wes also fell into the company of a mentor, the literally outsized George Crookham, an enormous man over sixty years old, who was outspoken in his opposition to alcohol and slavery, and a great lover of the outdoors. Crookham's schoolhouse, where he taught, contained a classroom on one side, and a museum of natural history on the other. Wes believed that his life was changed by his time with Crookham, as he and Crookham spent days riding around the county and visiting a geologist who lived nearby.[2]

As the issue of slavery grew more pronounced in the 1830s and 1840s, Wes's father Joseph became more strident in his opposition to the "peculiar institution." Joseph Powell subscribed to the *Oberlin Evangelist* and welcomed Oberlin faculty members and students into his home when they passed through Jackson. But this area of southern Ohio was not friendly to abolitionist thought. The Powell family became outcasts, enemies burned Crookham's schoolhouse to the ground, and in 1846 the Powells decided to move on to Wisconsin.[3]

After years of farming in Wisconsin, the Powells moved to Wheaton, Illinois, where Joseph became a trustee of the Illinois Institute, the forerunner of Wheaton College. Wes became a schoolteacher. He desired more education, though, and yearned to go to college. Ultimately he declined to enter the Illinois Institute and chose Illinois College instead, beginning in 1855.[4]

That summer before he began his studies, Wes bought a little skiff and headed upstream on the Mississippi River, camping as he went. It was a research trip for him—Powell collected mollusk shells and fossils all the way to St. Paul, Minnesota, from which he walked all the way across Wisconsin to Mackinac, Michigan. Then, having deposited his collections in the family home in Wheaton, Wes enrolled in the Scientific Program at Illinois College, which was a three-year course of study that excluded some of the language and theology requirements of the four-year degree. He joined a literary society, Sigma Pi, and engaged in the literary society debates. Even though his curriculum did not emphasize the natural sciences, at Illinois College Powell was gaining a heightened ability to formulate questions and organize his thoughts systematically. In the literary society debates, Powell thought through issues and employed evidence as the basis of his conclusions.[5]

After his first year at Illinois College, Powell taught school and then traveled alone the other direction on the Mississippi all the way to New Orleans. After another year at Illinois College, Powell continued his explorations. This time he set off from Pittsburgh and floated down the Ohio River to the mouth of the Wabash River, which he then traveled upstream into Indiana until he finally left the Wabash and trod his way to Michigan and the Great Lakes. Augmenting his college work, he schooled himself in the geography and natural history of the interior of the United States, watching the development of the country. Over the summer he went on yet another excursion, this time seeking minerals in the Iron Mountain area of Missouri.[6]

These trips, however, did not produce income, and Wes was not able to resume a third year at Illinois College. Instead, he lived at home in Wheaton and enrolled in the Illinois Institute, where numerous family members already attended. His parents would manage to provide some collegiate education for all eight of their children, a rare feat in that day. There, at this coeducational school, he joined the coeducational Beltionian Literary Society and soon became a leader of the group. But the Illinois Institute collegiate classes were only organized through the sophomore year, and in the spring, after only two terms, he withdrew and resumed his studies at yet another school, Oberlin College. Powell pursued his studies at Oberlin for only five months, and apparently spent a good part of this time outdoors. He then completed a partial year in a return to the Illinois Institute, but when he dropped out, with about three total years of collegiate education, he was leaving college ranks behind for good.[7]

That same year Powell joined the newly organized Natural History Society of Illinois, based at the State Normal University in Bloomington. His own collections had grown to include thousands of plants and shells, along with numerous reptiles. Soon, in January 1859, he took a job as a schoolteacher in northwestern Illinois, but through his membership in the Natural History Society he was connected to others of a like mind, and he had the opportunity to show off his own collections. When the census taker appeared in 1860, Powell identified his profession as "Naturalist."[8]

During the Civil War, Powell joined the Union Army and fought at Shiloh, where he lost most of his right arm. After the war, he resumed his teaching career, this time as a college professor. Though he was not a college graduate, Illinois Wesleyan University granted Powell an honorary M.A. degree, which then qualified him to join the faculty. He spent one year there, and then moved on to the Illinois State Normal University, from which he launched his explorations of the American West. Powell then made two trips down the Green and Colorado rivers, through the Grand Canyon, the first passes by European Americans, making the Western interior far more known than it ever had been before. In 1881 Powell became head of the United States Geological Survey, where he remained until 1894. He also directed the Smithsonian Bureau of Eth-nology.[9] Powell's life carried him far beyond the world he had known in southern Ohio, Wisconsin, Illinois, and in a variety of the institu-tions of higher education in the region as both student and professor. Yet the antebellum West was where he sparked his interests and forged his commitments.

A figure similar to Powell was Harvey W. Wiley, born in southern In-diana in 1844. His father was a farmer, plasterer, local schoolmaster, and an elder and pastor in the Disciples of Christ church. His mother made all of Harvey's clothing, and the family was highly self-sufficient. The parents believed in education. Despite their relative poverty, all three of Harvey's sisters went to college for at least one year (one at Antioch, the other two at North Western Christian University), and his eldest sister became one of the first female physicians in the United States.[10]

The Wiley family was pious and Calvinist, Harvey remembered: "strict observance of the Sabbath was one of the fundamentals of my bringing up. I was not allowed even to whistle on Sunday." Harvey's mother had been born in Kentucky near Cane Ridge. Her family had been part of Barton Warren Stone's church and were thus some of the initial Disciples of Christ church members. Harvey remembered about his youth that "debates were common in that day," and the Disciples of Christ were for-ever taking on believers of other denominations, sometimes in debates that "lasted several days, and waxed warm and eloquent."[11]

The Wileys were also abolitionists. Harvey remembered that when Harriet Beecher Stowe's *Uncle Tom's Cabin* was being published in serial form in the *National Era*, on Friday nights after supper Harvey's father "would read the story. Many were the tears we shed as the vivid narrative progressed. At the end of each reading father would read a chapter from the Bible and we would all kneel down for evening prayers. It is not dif-ficult to imagine that our whole family grew up with a feeling of bitter antagonism toward the institution of slavery."[12]

Harvey had a number of different schoolmasters, including one woman who had been a student at Antioch with his sister, and he had access to books through a library system in Indiana in which a "good selection of books was deposited with the trustee of each township, kept there a certain length of time, and then transferred to the next town-ship. In this way, in the course of a few years, every township in the state had access to all the standard works of history, fiction, literature, and other kindred educational topics." At the age of eighteen, in 1862, Harvey decided to go to Hanover College, not far from where he lived, and he walked there to enroll. In his impecunious state, he rented a tiny room and did not eat meat. On Saturdays he walked home, ate breakfast, then worked all day in his father's fields to earn money to defray his rent expenses. His wardrobe was still made by his mother.[13]

At Hanover, Harvey joined the Philalethean Literary Society. He explained, "The two literary societies were very important influences at Hanover. They met every Friday night. The exercises consisted of essays, declamations, and debates. All the members were regularly assigned during the year to one or more of these performances." The "greatest event of the school year" was the spring exhibition, and "[t]he audience was composed not only of students and citizens of the village, but people from all the countryside and from Madison came to these exhibitions." Wiley understood what a literary society was, and what it was not. When another student asked Harvey if he wanted to participate in a Greek-letter fraternity he was organizing, Wiley explained that he would like to, but could not, as "my father has always told me to avoid secret societies."[14]

At Hanover, Wiley received a sound education in science. The father in-law of Benjamin Harrison, John W. Scott, taught Wiley chemistry, and taught "also physics and botany and some other branches of the natural sciences, and he taught them all well." Wiley and a friend became "very much interested in botany at Hanover and we spent the time largely in botanizing along the banks of the Miami. I collected something of a herbarium of wild flowers and plants which my mother carefully preserved for me."[15]

Wiley was a member of the Indiana Legion, the home guard of the state, and in 1864 he left Hanover for a time, with many other students, to enlist for 100 days in the Union Army. After experiencing severe diarrhea and hookworm he was finally discharged. Months later he had recovered enough to resume his Hanover studies. In April 1865, Harvey recalled, "During the spring public performance of the Philalethean Society I read the first essay that was a precursor of my whole active career, an essay on health."[16]

Hanover was not a wealthy school, and Wiley later concluded "[p]overty has its uses in academic instruction as well as in the building of character. The teachers who have to struggle for existence, in my opinion, have a decided advantage over those who are pampered by large incomes, easy chairs and luxury which tends to deaden the finer instincts of the pedagogic profession. Hanover was a rich beneficiary of poverty. I carried away a fine heritage from personal contact with teachers and students."[17]

From these beginnings, Harvey Wiley became a schoolteacher in Indiana, and then a tutor in Latin and Greek at Northwestern Christian
University in Indianapolis, where he continued his medical studies at
the Indiana Medical College, after having read with and worked with a
doctor in Kentucky. Wiley graduated with his M.D. degree in 1871, and
when the Indiana Medical College wanted to hire him as their chemistry
professor he agreed, but only if they would let him continue his studies
before joining the faculty. At Midwestern meetings of the American Association for the Advancement of Science, Wiley had become acquainted
with some Harvard scientists, and he decided to study at Harvard, in the
Lawrence Scientific School. During the five months of his stay he heard
a series of lectures by John Tyndall and Louis Agassiz, among others,
and he then returned to Indiana. Soon he migrated to newly established
Purdue University where he taught chemistry for nine years, interrupted
by a year spent in Europe where he studied medicine, chemistry, physics,
and pathology. From this post at Purdue he became, in 1883, a federal
employee, chief chemist for the Department of Agriculture.[18]

It was in this capacity that Wiley made his most significant contributions to the nation through decades of work trying to protect consumers
from food adulteration. The high point of this work arrived in 1906 with
one of the signature accomplishments of the Progressive era, the creation
of the Food and Drug Administration.[19]

The importance of the Western denominational colleges to the
Progressive era was one of the significant findings of historian Robert
Crunden, who argued that "progressivism was a climate of creativity within which writers, artists, politicians, and thinkers functioned."
Crunden found that the "progressive personality" experienced "its birth
in the Middle West" because of the special experience of that region.
New England was too constricting to produce many people with the vision and creativity of the Progressives. Southerners did not have Abraham Lincoln as a hero, whereas in the Midwest, a generation of men and
women grew up in devout Protestant homes, judging themselves and
others with their model, Lincoln, as the standard.[20]

Often encouraged by family to go into the ministry, this generation instead went into the newer professions that enshrined altruism and public
service as high ideals, especially "journalism, settlement work, higher
education, law, or politics." They believed that because of the declining
status of the ministry, one could better serve God in these influential
professions. And these young Progressives found themselves most wel-
come in the Midwest, where they worked in "a relatively unstructured

intellectual and professional climate that encouraged new insights." Though they did not all go to college, the typical Progressive went to college at a small denominational school.[21]

These years were when the people living in Midwestern cities such as Chicago, St. Louis, Milwaukee, and Detroit recognized "a common heartland consciousness" and saw their cities as the hub of a great nation. The spectacle of Chicago's Columbian Exposition in 1893, the bustle of Detroit during the automobile revolution, the skyscrapers that rose to amazing heights, and the architectural styles being rethought by the likes of Louis Sullivan and Frank Lloyd Wright were testament to the vitality of Midwestern life and culture.[22]

In literature, these were the decades of the Midwestern ascendancy, when Carl Sandburg, Hamlin Garland, Theodore Dreiser, Willa Cather, Sherwood Anderson, Booth Tarkington, F. Scott Fitzgerald, and Sinclair Lewis published their finest work, and a generation of the most promising authors and poets were making their way to Chicago to hone their skills, hang out with Floyd Dell and Margery Curry, or join the Dill Pickle Club. When Lewis became the first American to win the Nobel Prize in literature in 1930, the award was indicative of the critical acclaim then accorded Midwestern literature.[23]

In the writing of history, Frederick Jackson Turner's address invoking the frontier thesis at the Columbian Exposition in 1893 inaugurated an era in which the major American historians, Turner, Charles Beard, Carl Becker, and Vernon Parrington, were Midwesterners. Historian David S. Brown, focused on Turner, Beard, William Appleman Williams, Merle Curti, and Christopher Lasch, has described a Midwestern school of thought about domestic and foreign policy that lasted at least to the end of the twentieth century. Rooted in an egalitarian, populist, and Progressive mindset that rejected American imperialism and unrestrained capitalism, these historians found hope for American democracy beyond the coastal metropolises.[24]

Invention was another area in which Midwesterners excelled. Thomas Edison had come from the West in an earlier era, but the late nineteenth century was filled with Midwesterners who created new things. In 1900, Dayton, Ohio, had the highest number of patents per capita of any American city, an indication of the future-minded dynamism of the period.[25]

Many of Dayton's patents were the responsibility of people who worked for John Patterson, the head of National Cash Register. When Patterson learned that a bar was going to open in a building near his factories, he preempted the plan by purchasing the building himself and made it into a chapel, a meeting place for his employees, and a kindergarten for their children. Action of this sort was not uncommon for Patterson, who personified Progressive Era corporate welfare notions, but the name of the house is significant—Patterson called it "the House of Usefulness."[26]

Two of Dayton's greatest inventors were Orville and Wilbur Wright. Neither Wilbur nor Orville went to college, but they grew up in the home of their father, Bishop Milton Wright. Wright had been born in Rush County, Indiana, in 1828. The family was devout, with a number of religious influences upon it. Milton attended public schools and also delved deeply into the books available in the public library. He loved debate, and would practice his speeches as he worked in the fields on the family farm.[27]

Milton heard preachers representing several denominations. Theologically, he warmed to the Methodists, but their lack of antislavery convictions and their search for popularity ruled them out. Eventually he found a home among the United Brethren, who were "respectable, but not cursed with popularity," and joined in 1847.[28]

Soon Milton felt a call to ministry, and the United Brethren made him an "exhorter," which allowed him to follow a preacher's sermon with his own call for repentance and conversion. Milton continued on this path, and in 1852 the White River Conference licensed him to preach. He practiced preaching alone outdoors, and he joined a debate society to hone his speaking skills. Milton also studied for ministry by reading diligently. In 1854 he wrote in a letter how much he wished for various books, including "a dictionary, an arithmetic book, Lyman Beecher's *Lectures*, Milton's *Paradise Lost*, a chemistry book, and a book on elocution."[29]

During these years, from 1849 to 1855, Milton Wright supported himself by teaching school. In 1853, he taught in the Preparatory school that was part of Hartsville University, a newly established United Brethren school in southern Indiana. Besides teaching his students, Wright took a collegiate course in Greek, but illness prevented him from continuing his studies. He returned to teaching elsewhere, and then became a United Brethren minister, preaching the gospel to his parishioners and adhering to a social code of opposition to alcohol, slavery, and secret societies. He worked in Indiana as a minister most of the time, including work as editor of religious newspapers and another stint at Hartsville University as a professor in the late 1860s and early 1870s, but also spent years before that on the Oregon frontier, heading a school called Sublimity College and preaching constantly.[30]

In time, Milton Wright married and had a family that included his sons Wilbur and Orville. For all of his children he supported excellent education, including access to a home library of high quality. Milton kept his theology library upstairs in his bedroom, and his children could read those books, but downstairs was the family library, stocked with fairy tales, British and American literature, and writings of classical authors such as Plutarch, Plato, and Socrates, as well as standard reference works. Wright explained that he opposed "intellectual slavery," in which children were forced to adopt their parents' way of thinking, and he prized "independent thought" in all things. As Milton put it, "Young man, young lady,—strike for independence—*think for yourselves*." After Orville Wright's accomplishments were manifest in the public mind, someone observed to Orville and Wilbur that they were representatives of that class of people who accomplished great things without "special advantages." Orville replied that to the contrary, "We were lucky enough to grow up in a home environment where there was always much encouragement to children to pursue intellectual interests; to investigate whatever aroused curiosity. In a different kind of environment our curiosity might have been nipped long before it could have borne fruit."[31]

This period, the Progressive era, is also when the Middle West became a region in the American mind. Cultural geographer James R. Shortridge has explained that by 1898 people thought of Kansas and Nebraska as the Middle West, and only in the early twentieth century did people expand their definition of the Middle West to include a broader expanse of territory. Shortridge found that, between 1902 and 1912, more and more people used the term to apply to a broad portion of the interior of the continent. By 1912 there was general agreement among Americans that the "Middle West" (or "Midwest," as it was often referred to beginning in 1918), included the states of the Old Northwest (Ohio, Michigan, Indiana, Illinois, and Wisconsin), along with Minnesota, Iowa, Missouri, North and South Dakota, Nebraska, and Kansas.[32] The Progressive movement, which reached its peak during these years, was the impetus for the designation of this regional term. Something was happening in the middle of the country, and people needed an appellation to describe it.

One of the key values of the Progressives was a belief in science. Unsurprisingly, Midwesterners were numerous in this area. In 1952, R. H. Knapp and H. B. Goodrich published research on the baccalaureate background of 18,000 American scientists of the late nineteenth and twentieth centuries. Their most striking finding was that an outright majority of the top fifty schools most productive of graduates who went on to obtain Ph.D.'s in science were located in the Midwest. Astonishingly, eight of the top fifty schools were in Ohio, and the majority of the rest extended further into the Midwest and the far West in a shotgun blast pattern that made Ohio look like a cultural hearth. A few public or research universities made the list, but the vast majority of the schools were denominationally founded liberal arts colleges, "many of limited reputation."[33]

Knapp and Goodrich came to a variety of conclusions. The American South was distinctly unproductive of scientists, which Knapp and Goodrich attributed to the Southern tendency to maintain a classical curriculum. In other regions, there was more devotion to science in the curriculum and to fine facilities for the study of science. Yet at Mid-Atlantic and New England schools, despite the resources expended on scientific instruction, and despite students who were often of high academic caliber, the proportion of students who went on to become scientists was much lower than in the Midwest and Far West. Knapp and Goodrich concluded that class was an important factor. At Mid-Atlantic and New England schools, the students did not see becoming a scientist as a vocation that would lift them socioeconomically. Many times their backgrounds were such that they had more prestigious or lucrative careers open to them in other areas. As Steven Shapin has observed, "[a]n appreciation that a life in science was *not* a fit way of making a bourgeois living persisted in America well into the twentieth century."[34]

In the Midwest, and even the Far West, however, many of the students came from "middle-class or lower-middle-class families and from smaller centers of population and semi-rural areas." Knapp and Goodrich theorized that for these students, a career as a scientist was a step up on the socioeconomic ladder. One professor remarked to the investigators that for many of his students, the choice was literally between the test tube and the plow.[35]

Another factor was that Eastern college leaders often kept the natural sciences at arm's length. The example of Yale is revealing. There, scientific studies commenced in 1846 in the Sheffield Scientific School, but the school was explicitly for the instruction of students who were not Yale undergraduates. These Easterners had a great aversion to mixing what they saw as the pure study of the classics with the practical education of science. Similar differences existed at Harvard and at Dartmouth and elsewhere through much of the nineteenth century in ways that communicated to students the undesirability of a life of scientific inquiry.[36]

By way of contrast, the antebellum culture of the West contributed to this later stream of scientists from the Midwest and the Rocky Mountain and Pacific West. As already discussed, manual labor in the 1850s was becoming a form of scientific agriculture, and forms of manual labor reappeared in the Land Grant universities of the late nineteenth century. From these efforts at scientific agriculture, it was only a small step further to the laboratory and the training of scientists.

Unlike the study of the classics, in which cultural elites stood as gatekeepers and allowed those whom they wished to learn the languages and the truths of the ancients, anyone who understood the scientific method could make discoveries, without necessarily having access to a particular library or course of study. Like manual labor, scientific inquiry was both hands-on and productive—it often resulted in things that were useful. Moreover, in the nineteenth century, Kim Tolley has argued, most Americans viewed scientific study as a female discipline, as opposed to the study of the classics, so thoroughly aligned with masculine culture. In the East, scientific study remained set apart from the standard curriculum, but in the West, scientific study became integrated with the collegiate curriculum and connoted different ideas about gender and status.[37]

In the Midwest, with its emphasis on productive work, students gravitated to disciplines in which they would gather specimens, dissect animals, and dig up rocks. The desire to be useful threw students naturally into these scientific disciplines that promised both intellectual stimulation and societal benefits. From their nonelite origins, the vocation of science still called them, not to leave behind their backgrounds, but to utilize their interests in a culturally acceptable, even admirable, fashion. A region that prized experimentation naturally produced graduates in disciplines that constantly asked them to experiment, to test new ideas, and gather results. Here was one outgrowth of the manual labor movement, the pietistic emphasis on usefulness, and the egalitarianism of the region.[38]

Thus, Robert Noyce followed a well-worn path, one integrated with Midwestern regional culture. An examination of the scientists to whom Noyce was most closely tied demonstrates these connections to the educational norms that began in the antebellum Western colleges. At almost the same time that Noyce invented the integrated circuit, Jack Kilby, of Texas Instruments, independently created his own version of the integrated circuit. Kilby, born in Missouri, grew up in towns in Kansas and graduated from the University of Illinois, from which both of his parents had taken their degrees. As Kilby himself put it, "I grew up among the industrious descendants of the western settlers of the American Great Plains." His was a family of readers. Kilby was surrounded by books and magazines. He later concluded, "If you want your kids to grow up to be inventors, read them fairy tales." His boyhood included membership in the Boy Scouts and attendance at the first National Jamboree, held in Washington, D.C., in 1937. In high school, among other activities, he played football and basketball, played trombone in band, presided over his high school camera club, and worked on the yearbook staff.[39] It was a world Robert Noyce would have recognized.

Noyce's professor, Grant Gale, studied at the University of Wisconsin with John Bardeen, and it was John Bardeen and Walter Brattain, with William Shockley as their supervisor, who invented the transistor and solid-state electronics. John Bardeen's father was an administrator and physician with a great interest in public health who created a teaching hospital at the University of Wisconsin. His mother was an only child whose own mother died young. She fled her father's control where they lived in eastern Pennsylvania and studied art in New York and Chicago before joining the faculty of John Dewey's Laboratory School at the University of Chicago. There, she taught home economics. She explained that in her teaching philosophy, "Thinking does not occur for its own sake; it is not an end in itself. It arises from the need of meeting some difficulty, in reflecting upon the best way of overcoming it, and thus leads to planning, to projecting mentally the end to be reached, and deciding upon the steps necessary." Here was the emphasis on practical and hands-on experience so prized by Dewey and so in line with the regional priorities. This teacher imbued her son, John, with the same ideas about the links between thought and action. John Bardeen grew up in this altruistic family with a commitment to service. He was a Boy Scout who sang in an Episcopalian church youth choir, he built radios and set up a small laboratory in his basement, and his parents enrolled him in a high school run by the University of Wisconsin that was quite similar to the Dewey school in Chicago.[40]

Bardeen's partners in invention were Walter Brattain and William Shockley, both Pacific Westerners born to mothers who had attended coeducational colleges—Brattain's mother attended Whitman College before her graduation from Miles College, and Shockley's Unitarian mother majored in piano and art at Stanford. Their mothers were like Noyce's mother, and her mother, who had both graduated from Oberlin College.[41]

The transistor that Bardeen, Brattain, and Shockley created replaced an earlier invention, the vacuum tube, created by Lee De Forest. De Forest was a native Iowan born in 1873 whose mother had graduated from

MAP 2. Fifty institutions leading in production of scientists.

Iowa (later Grinnell) College. De Forest's father, an Iowan and Congregationalist minister, accepted a position in Alabama as head of Talladega College, a school for blacks. Because area whites were hostile to the family and because Lee De Forest was not accepted by blacks, either, he grew up mostly influenced by his Midwestern parents.[42]

These scientists and inventors came from families connected to the regional culture of the West that promoted education and coeducation, and was so closely tied to Protestantism and the Midwestern regional values—usefulness, productivity, egalitarianism. We should not be surprised to find, as Tom Wolfe has related, that it was scientists and engineers from the towns of the Midwest and the West who accomplished the achievements of the American space program in the 1960s. The influence of the antebellum West extended not just to Silicon Valley, but into outer space.[4]

* * *

When historian Arthur Bestor tried to explain why antebellum communitarian and utopian groups appeared in Western states at rates much higher than elsewhere, Bestor concluded that Westerners were inclined to found such societies because they "possessed a powerful sense of the plasticity of American institutions." Unburdened of the accumulated weight of precedent, these people believed they could purposefully create the sort of society in which they wished to live. In this region, institutional structures supported patterns of innovative thinking and encouraged receptivity to new ideas.[44]

Bestor's conclusions match what contemporaries claimed about the West. In 1833, transcendentalist James Freeman Clarke, who would go on to encourage the adoption of coeducation at Harvard, found "the West to be a place where freedom of thought prevails. I say things constantly with effect that if lisped in New England would be overborne at once by the dominant opinions." Years later, Albert Barnes, a New England minister interested in higher education, agreed and connected this characteristic to the institutional structure of Western life. Barnes claimed that while Easterners were connected to established institutions, "the western mind . . . is unsettled. . . . It is, to a great extent, broken off from old fixtures and associations, and new affinities and attachments are not yet formed." Westerners, argued Barnes, were "prepared for any new influences that may meet them."[45]

Westerners tended to talk about the lack of specialization in their region as a virtue. Witness the ideas of Daniel Drake, a notable scientist, physician, and educational leader in the West. In 1834, Drake addressed the members of the Union Literary Society of Miami University on the "history, Character, and Prospects of the West." Drake spoke about how educational environments shaped persons. Children "born in old and compactly organized communities," observed Drake, were "surrounded" by books, good schools with fine teachers, "ingenious toys," and "public lectures in lyceums." As a result, Drake argued, these children became "the objects of a sleepless superintendence" that "lays down the rules by which their growth in intellect shall proceed." These children would "acquire a copious and varied learning," and as adults display "a conformity more or less striking."[46] Drake's characterization of the educational process in long-settled areas was at once complimentary and critical. Drake did not deny the advantages, but he also portrayed the resulting adults of this educational process as conformists, overly bound by laws.

In contrast, Drake posited that the children of a "new country" had different opportunities. In the new country, the "want of arts and inventions" to solve problems led people to "invent and substitute others," which engendered "a spirit of independence." Drake cited the "many opportunities for bold enterprize" and argued that the problems people faced "call forth ingenuity." A lack of specialization was a marked characteristic of the West; while the Westerner would not attain the degree of perfection of the specialist, the varied demands of the West expanded the intellect. This same theme of the Westerner as unspecialized received a more extended exposition in 1838 from Andrew Wylie, who told his audience at Wabash College that the "division of labor . . . affords some striking illustrations of the effect which confinement to a narrow circle of thought has in producing mental imbecility." Wylie offered the example of a mechanic whose life consisted of pointing pins. Place the specialized mechanic alongside "the most unlettered, uncouth stripling you can find in the woods of Indiana," put the two of them in a predicament, and one would see who was more *"liberally educated."*

> The man of pins is confounded and paralized. But the Hoosier, who has rambled over mountain and forest, and met, every day of his life, with some new object to awaken his attention, or some new adventure to sharpen his wit, and who . . . has tried his hand at almost everything, . . . gathers up his thoughts in a moment, and . . . extricates both himself and his astounded companion.[47]

Wylie and Drake agreed that the West provided the most liberal of educations.

Significantly, Drake connected the liberal learning of the Westerner to the institutional structure of the region. Institutionally, the West lacked "the restraints employed by an old social organization." Drake told his listeners that "a thousand corporations,—literary, charitable, political, religious, and commercial, have not combined into an oligarchy" to erect "one set of artificial and traditional standards." As a result, in the West one found more "exhibitions of original character."[48]

At times Drake spoke romantically of the expanding influence of nature upon the intellect, but he also presented the Westerner as an empiricist, with a mind "favorable to the reception of new truths." The Miami University students listened as Drake told them that "the West is pre-eminently the place where discoveries and new principles of every kind, are received with avidity, and promptly submitted to the test of experiment." The inhabitants of the West fostered exposure to new ideas by the very fact that the Westerners themselves were a varied lot, "the enterprising and ambitious from other realms; and each has been a schoolmaster to our native population—presenting them with strange manners and customs; arts, opinions, and prejudices, not seen before."[49]

These people were at times hyperbolic in their rhetoric, yet we should recognize that they were saying many things in common. The ways Westerners built their colleges, and the ways Midwesterners defined the

Progressive era, and the ways people like Orville Wright and Jack Kilby talked about the intellectual environment in which they prospered, shows that something regionally distinctive happened in that place. The antebellum Western colleges manifested some of these ideas. In other cases, the antebellum booster rhetoric served as a set of ideals that many Westerners took seriously and attempted to incorporate into their lives and their institutions.

Wylie and Drake described key elements of an emerging Western culture in the 1830s. The Western college founders and professors included many of these elements in their educational structure and offerings in ways that afforded their students an education that was regionally distinct and perhaps especially conducive to scientific inquiry, in ways that equipped young men and women for experimentation, investigation, and invention. With ideas nurtured, cultivated, amplified, and broadcast by the colleges, people such as John Wesley Powell, Harvey W. Wiley, and Milton Wright carried the values of the region and its colleges into the Progressive era. And in the decades that followed, other inheritors of that Western regional culture left their stamp in wide-ranging places.

Conclusion

This book tells a story of one of many Midwests, a Midwest that counters both popular perceptions of the Midwest as bland and indistinct, and scholarly interpretations that mostly present the Midwest as having effloresced in the middle nineteenth century only thereafter to languish and stagnate. In the introduction to *The American Midwest: Essays on Regional History* (2001), the editors asked:

> How was it . . . that the place widely seen as the cutting edge of Western civilization in 1800 came to be perceived as a cultural cul-de-sac by the early 1900s? How, only decades after the region had exemplified reform and innovation, had Main Street and Middletown arisen to silence radicals, dissidents, and social critics, or drive them into exile? And why did the ideal of republican independence that nurtured Eugene V. Debs come to support the conformity of George F. Babbitt?[1]

Critics of the region frequently invoke Sinclair Lewis's *Main Street* (1920) and *Babbitt* (1922) as proof, from a native Midwesterner, no less, that the Midwest regressed from a once creative and vibrant culture to a crass, complacent shell of its former complexity. To be sure, *Babbitt* is important because some people in the region had given up the regional culture of the nineteenth and early twentieth centuries. Lewis wrote that George Babbitt "made nothing in particular, neither butter nor shoes nor poetry"—Babbitt, tragically, had missed his call to productivity and usefulness. Babbitt barely thought of the sacred and divine. He was instead "a pious motorist," in love with automobiles, but uninterested, except in snatches of dreams, in transcendence or dignifying the human condition.[2]

Critics of the Midwest, however, pay little attention to one of Lewis's most significant books. *Arrowsmith*, published in 1924, won a Pulitzer Prize. The novel is about a small-town Midwestern man who, over the course of his life, embraced a self-sacrificial dedication to medicine and science as a form of service to humankind. Though *Arrowsmith* satirized anti-intellectualism and vapid boosterism, Lewis also celebrated the cultural legacy of the Midwest, its embrace of productive curiosity, its willingness to search for new solutions to problems, its democratic ethos. Scholars who miss the significance of *Arrowsmith* do so because they discount the possibility that there are "many Midwests," that Eugene Debs and George Babbitt are not contradictory; rather, they were contemporaries.[3]

The novel begins with "a ragged girl of fourteen" driving a wagon "through forest and swamp of the Ohio wilderness." Her mother is dead, her younger siblings need care, and her feverish father suggests that they go to Cincinnati to find a relative. She rejects her father's advice: "'We're going on jus' long as we can. Going West! They's a whole lot of new things I aim to be seeing!' She cooked the supper, she put the children to bed, and sat by the fire, alone. That," explained Lewis, "was the great-grandmother of Martin Arrowsmith."[4]

Having established the spunky ancestry of Arrowsmith, Lewis explains that Martin grew up in the Midwestern village of Elk Mills, and went to a small university, where he forswore joining a fraternity because "he had resented the condescension of the aristocracy of men from the larger cities." He worked hard at his studies, and during summers he worked at manual labor: "That summer he spent with a crew installing telephones in Montana. He was a linesman in the wire-gang," wrote Lewis. "Martin wore overalls and a flannel shirt. He looked like a farm-hand. . . . The wire-gang were as healthy and as simple as the west wind; they had no pretentiousness."[5]

On campus, Martin fell in love with scientific investigation as a search for truth, though "he saw no one clear path to Truth but a thousand paths to a thousand truths far-off and doubtful." He went through medical school and became a country doctor, but resisted the call of "commercialism" and remained true to his desire to do scientific experiments that would lead to the betterment of society. Martin had his share of human foibles and weaknesses, but he "had one gift: curiosity whereby he saw nothing as ordinary." Ultimately he avoided the "men of measured merriment" who sought positive public relations more than a search for truth or to alleviate human suffering. Arrowsmith advanced in his career to the prestigious McGurk Center in New York, and then took the results of his experimentation to an island where an outbreak of the plague was killing people. At great risk to his own life, and despite the death of his devoted wife Leora, he worked heroically to save people's lives. He chose to be useful.[6]

For Lewis, Martin Arrowsmith represented a continuation of the spirit of the early settlers of the trans-Appalachian West. His egalitarian nature and admiration of productive labor marked him as a Midwesterner. Many people inside and outside the region read this novel. In 1931, two soon-to-be Hollywood legends, producer Samuel Goldwyn and director John Ford, translated the novel's popularity into box office success and earned a nomination for "Best Picture" with their film by the same title. Steven Shapin, a leading scholar of American science, has discovered that *Arrowsmith*, through its "hero as scientist" tale, inspired numerous Americans to embrace a life of scientific inquiry. And as late as 1961, *Arrowsmith* was still the most widely read of Lewis's novels. Yet a half century later, few people invoke *Arrowsmith* any longer. *The American Midwest: An Interpretive Encyclopedia*, published in 2007, indexed five references to *Babbitt* and eleven to *Main Street*, including an essay specifically about those two books. The encyclopedia made no reference to *Arrowsmith*. Lewis's novel about a Progressive-era scientist from the Midwest was no longer part of a narrative of Midwestern history, no longer seen as a clue to the meaning of the region.[7]

Some scholars have overlooked *Arrowsmith* in part because of the rise of the East Coast intellectual establishment. Warren Susman found that in the 1920s urban, East Coast intellectuals revolted against "what was considered to be the Midwestern domination of American life and values." The response to the publication in 1920 of *Main Street* underscores Susman's observations. Conventional wisdom holds that *Main Street* attacked the provincial and stultifying nature of the small town. But Lewis also praised the natural beauty, the farmers who lived near Main Street, and Will Kennicott, who was a steady, dutiful, humane man. In a letter written shortly after publication of *Main Street* Lewis wrote, "If I didn't love Main Street would I write of it so hotly? could I write of it so ragingly?" Authors, however, do not control the reception to what they write, and the response to *Main Street* and *Babbitt* showed that the image of the Midwest had changed in the American mind.[8]

In the middle twentieth century, Richard Hofstadter, a professor of history at Columbia University, continued the revolt against the Midwest. At a time when Joseph McCarthy, the rabidly anticommunist senator from Wisconsin, held so much dangerous power, Hofstadter channeled the anxieties of the antebellum New England supporters of the Western Education Society. Hofstadter disparaged the antebellum period of college building as "the Great Retrogression." With various co-authors, he described the antebellum colleges as "feckless" institutions "in various stages of inanition." The Americans "weakly founded" far too many colleges, which led to stunning failure rates of 80 percent. Even surviving colleges "were frequently too small to be educationally effective; they lacked complexity, they lacked variety." The professors were "uninspired" and "backward" in their teaching methods, and because the "provincial colleges" of "the West and South" were not attuned to the changing nation, the education students gained was not useful.[9]

Hofstadter presented the growth of the antebellum college through the metaphor of disease and madness. "The great retrogression," insisted Hofstadter, "was in good part the outcome of the epidemic of revivals, the rise of fundamentalism, and the all but unchecked ragings of the denominational spirit." These forces, in combination with "feverish local rivalries," led to "denomination-ridden, poverty-stricken" colleges, "full of episodes of almost hysterical rebellion." Hofstadter abhorred the institutional abolitionism of Oberlin College, for example, as an affront to academic freedom. Yet Hofstadter could give thanks that even though the leaders and supporters of the small denominational colleges "tried to cripple or destroy" improved forms of higher education, during the late nineteenth and early twentieth centuries an "educational revolution" took place in which the modern, secular university became the dominant force in American higher education. Research now ranked equally with teaching, and "methods and concepts of science displaced the authority of religion." Hofstadter dichotomized religion and science, denominational college and secular university, and posited a disjuncture between the antebellum college and the modern university.[10]

It may seem strange that Hofstadter's ideas would need refutation or rejoinder at this point. Yet as Alan Brinkley wrote in 1985 of Hofstadter's *The Age of Reform*, "It is a book whose central interpretations few historians any longer accept, but one whose influence few historians can escape," notwithstanding "a strikingly thin acquaintance with the sources." Hofstadter viewed with suspicion the forces of "reaction" within the Populist and Progressive movements that existed "particularly in the

Middle West and the South," and it is difficult to escape the conclusion that he had a skeptical view of the Midwest as a region during almost the whole of American history.[11] Hofstadter still shapes the way scholars view antebellum American higher education, and indirectly, the ways we think about the history and meaning of the Midwest.

Recently many people interested in regionalism have put their emphasis on "state of mind" and "sense of place," sometimes discounting where people were on a map. As Andrew Cayton wrote in 2001, "economic, social, and political structures matter only tangentially in the construction of regionalism; what is real does not matter much at all."[12] Yet regionalism does not emerge out of thin air or imaginings divorced from physical realities. Rather, regionalism is precisely the dialectic between thought and action, between the imagined and the tangible.

Antebellum Western college founders wanted to fill up their region with colleges. They knew that their manual labor programs matched the desires and needs of people in that place. These founders created coeducational colleges because they were dedicated to usefulness and had different conceptions of gender boundaries than college founders in other regions. The Western colleges had priorities and a campus culture that reflected the values of their professors and students. Over time, the ethos of the antebellum Western colleges was deeply connected to Progressivism and American science, to Robert Noyce, the microchip, and the birth of Silicon Valley. Martin Arrowsmith would have recognized that Midwest, for it was the Midwest he inherited and in which he lived.

Notes

Introduction

1. Leslie Berlin, *The Man Behind the Microchip: Robert Noyce and the Invention of Silicon Valley* (New York: Oxford University Press, 2005), 7–14.

2. Tom Wolfe, "Two Young Men Who Went West," in *Hooking Up* (New York: Farrar, Straus, and Giroux, 2000), 19–25; Berlin, *The Man Behind the Microchip*, 14–27.

3. Wolfe, "Two Young Men Who Went West," 26–36, 47–50; T. R. Reid, *The Chip: How Two Americans Invented the Microchip and Launched a Revolution* (New York: Random House, 1985); Jeffrey Zygmont, *Microchip: An Idea, Its Genesis, and the Revolution It Created* (Cambridge, MA: Perseus, 2003).

4. Wolfe, "Two Young Men Who Went West," 38–43, 50–55. AnnaLee Saxenian accepts and buttresses Wolfe's interpretation in her comparative study of the differences in corporate cultures. The Route 128 area in Massachusetts was a leading area in electronics technologies during much of the latter half of the twentieth century, but was eclipsed by Silicon Valley. Saxenian found that the corporate culture of the Silicon Valley, far more decentralized and less rigid and hierarchical, accounted for much of the difference. AnnaLee Saxenian, *Regional Advantage: Culture and Competition in Silicon Valley and Route 128* (Cambridge: Harvard University Press, 1994).

5. Historians frequently and appropriately refer to the area north of the Ohio River during the antebellum period as the Midwest, but I will describe the place, as contemporaries did, as the West. This area was especially the territory formed from the Northwest Ordinance of 1787 that later became the Old Northwest—Ohio, Michigan, Indiana, Illinois, and Wisconsin—as well as Iowa. During my discussion of the late nineteenth and early twentieth centuries, I use the term "Midwest" to describe a broader region that included the states of the Old Northwest and Minnesota, Iowa, most of Missouri, and the eastern portions of the Dakotas, Nebraska, and Kansas.

Most Americans in the late eighteenth and early nineteenth centuries described the Ohio River Valley as the "West," and often included Kentucky until the 1840s and 1850s. On the boundaries of the "West," see Kenneth H. Wheeler, "Higher Education in the Antebellum Ohio Valley: Slavery, Sectionalism, and the Erosion of Regional Identity," *Ohio Valley History* 8 (Spring 2008): 1–22. See also Henry Nash Smith, *Virgin Land: The American West as a Symbol and Myth* (Cambridge: Harvard University Press, 1950), 122–132; Stephen Aron, *How the West Was Lost: The Transformation of Kentucky from Daniel Boone to Henry Clay* (Baltimore: Johns Hopkins University Press, 1996); and Kim M. Gruenwald, "Space and Place on the Early American Frontier: The Ohio Valley as a Region, 1790–1850," *Ohio Valley History* 4 (Fall 2004): 31–48. On the origins of the term "Middle West," see James R. Shortridge, *The Middle West: Its Meaning in American Culture* (Lawrence: University Press of Kansas, 1989), 13–26.

6. Standard histories of American higher education include John S. Brubacher and Willis Rudy, *Higher Education in Transition: A History of American Colleges and Universities, 1636–1958* (New York: Harper & Row, 1958); Frederick Rudolph, *The American College and University: A History* (New York: Knopf, 1962); Lawrence A. Cremin, *American Education: The National Experience, 1783–1876* (New York: Harper and Row, 1980); Christopher J. Lucas, *American Higher Education: A History* (New York: St. Martin's Press, 1994); and John R. Thelin, *A History of American Higher Education* (Baltimore: The Johns Hopkins University Press, 2004).

Names of schools at the time were not standardized, thus higher education included schools that were called variously "universities," "colleges," "collegiate institutes," "institutes," "academies," and "seminaries." I have limited my investigation almost exclusively to schools that offered collegiate-level studies and were recognized as colleges at that time, even if the college existed in conjunction with an academy or seminary. See the appendices in Colin B. Burke, *American Collegiate Populations: A Test of the Traditional View* (New York: New York University Press, 1982). A growing literature documents schools of "higher learning" throughout the nation during that period. See, for example, Nancy Beadie and Kim Tolley, eds. *Chartered Schools: Two Hundred Years of Independent Academies in the United States, 1727–1925* (New York: RoutledgeFalmer, 2002); and Margaret A. Nash, *Women's Education in the United States, 1780–1840* (New York: Palgrave Macmillan, 2005).

7. Historians of American higher education once argued that these Western colleges were not of lasting significance, a temporary "Great Retrogression," as Richard Hofstadter put it. Though historians have since debunked these ideas, an assertion of what these colleges meant has been lacking, despite calls from historians for studies of regionalism within American higher education. For the now-debunked critique of Western colleges, see Donald G. Tewksbury, *The Founding of American Colleges and Universities Before the Civil War: With Particular Reference to the Religious Influences Bearing Upon the College Movement* (New York: Archon Books, 1965 [1932]); Richard Hofstadter and C. DeWitt Hardy, *The Development and Scope of Higher Education in the United States* (New York: Columbia University Press, 1952), 19; Richard Hofstadter, "The Revolution in Higher Education," 269–290, in Arthur M. Schlesinger, Jr., and Morton White, eds. *Paths of American Thought* (Boston: Houghton Mifflin Company, 1963), 269–271; Richard Hofstadter and Walter P. Metzger, *The Development of Academic Freedom in the United States* (New York: Columbia University Press, 1955), 214–215; and Richard Hofstadter and Wilson Smith, eds. *American Higher Education: A Documentary History*, 2 vols. (Chicago: University of Chicago Press, 1961).

The debunkers include Natalie Naylor, "The Antebellum College Movement: A Reappraisal of Tewksbury's Founding of American Colleges and Universities," *History of Education Quarterly* 13 (1973): 261–274; and James Axtell, "The Death of the Liberal Arts College," *History of Education Quarterly* 11 (1971): 339–352. For other scholarship in this same vein, see also Daniel J. Boorstin, *The Americans: The National Experience* (New York: Vintage Books, 1965), esp. 152–161; David B. Potts, "American Colleges in the Nineteenth Century: From Localism to Denominationalism," *History of Education Quarterly* 11 (1971): 363–380; Timothy L. Smith, "Uncommon Schools: Christian Colleges and Social Idealism in Midwestern America, 1820–1950," in *Indiana Historical Society Lectures, 1976–1977: The History of Education in the Middle West* (Indianapolis: Indiana Historical Society, 1978); James McLachlan, "The American College in the Nineteenth Century: Toward a Reappraisal," *Teachers College Record* 80 (1978): 287–306; and Burke, *American Collegiate Populations*.

On the need for regional studies of nineteenth-century higher education, see Roger L. Geiger, "Introduction: New Themes in the History of Nineteenth-Century Colleges," in Roger Geiger, ed. *The American College in the Nineteenth Century* (Nashville, TN: Vanderbilt University Press, 2000), 1–36. The most important regional studies published to date include David F. Allmendinger, Jr., *Paupers and Scholars: The Transformation of Student Life in Nineteenth-Century New England* (New York: St. Martin's Press, 1975); Smith, "Uncommon Schools"; Robert F. Pace, *Halls of Honor: College Men in the Old South* (Baton Rouge: Louisiana State University Press, 2004); and Jennifer R. Green, *Military Education and the Emerging Middle Class in the Old South* (New York: Cambridge University Press, 2008).

My interpretation differs from the trajectory and the central values of the region ascribed by other historians. See, for example, Andrew R. L. Cayton and Peter S. Onuf, *The Midwest and the Nation: Rethinking the History of an American Region* (Bloomington: Indiana University Press, 1990); Andrew R. L. Cayton and Susan Gray, eds. *The American Midwest: Essays on Regional History* (Bloomington: Indiana University Press, 2001), esp. 3; and Andrew R. L. Cayton, "General Overview," in Richard Sisson, Christian Zacher, and Andrew Cayton, eds. *The American Midwest: An Interpretive Encyclopedia* (Bloomington: Indiana University Press, 2007), esp. xxii, xix.

8. R. H. Knapp and H. B. Goodrich, *Origins of American Scientists* (Chicago: University of Chicago Press, 1952), esp. 22–24.

9. For the leading theorist of imagined communities, see Benedict R. O'G. Anderson, *Imagined Communities: Reflections on the Origin and Spread of Nationalism* (London: Verso, 1983). For an example of a similar approach to understanding culture through an examination of higher education, see J. David Hoeveler, *Creating the American Mind: Intellect and Politics in the Colonial Colleges* (Lanham, MD: Rowman & Littlefield, 2002).

1 / Building Western Colleges

1. The best accounting of antebellum colleges in each state is found in Colin B. Burke, *American Collegiate Populations: A Test of the Traditional View* (New York: New York University Press, 1982), 299–318.

2. Eric Hinderaker, *Elusive Empires: Constructing Colonialism in the Ohio Valley, 1673–1800* (New York: Cambridge University Press, 1997); Beverley W. Bond, Jr., *The Civilization of the Old Northwest: A Study of Political, Social, and Economic Development, 1788–1812* (New York: The Macmillan Company, 1934); R. Carlyle Buley, *The Old Northwest: Pioneer Period, 1815–1840*, 2 vols. (Bloomington: Indiana University

Press, 1950), esp. 1:1–138; Andrew R. L. Cayton and Peter S. Onuf, *The Midwest and the Nation: Rethinking the History of an American Region* (Bloomington: Indiana University Press, 1990), esp. Chapter 2, "The Peopling of the Old Northwest," 25–42; and Andrew R. L. Cayton, "The Middle West," in William L. Barney, ed. *A Companion to 19th-Century America* (Malden, MA: Blackwell Publishing, 2001), 272–285, esp. 275–276.

3. G. M. Beswick to Asbury Wilkinson, June 30, 1846, Box 1, Folder 2, Asbury Wilkinson Papers, M 295, Indiana Historical Society, Indianapolis; Nathan O. Hatch, *The Democratization of American Christianity* (New Haven: Yale University Press, 1989).

4. On the implementation of the Land Ordinance of 1785, see Payson Jackson Treat, *The National Land System, 1785–1820* (New York: E. B. Treat & Company, 1910). The notable exceptions to the rectangular system of survey in the Western states north of the Ohio occurred in the Virginia Military District in southern Ohio, and in the much smaller Clark's Grant area of southern Indiana. Bond, *The Civilization of the Old Northwest*, 6. On settlement patterns and survey methods, see Norman J. W. Thrower, *Original Survey and Land Subdivision: A Comparative Study of the Form and Effect of Contrasting Cadastral Surveys* (Chicago: Rand McNally & Co., 1966), esp. 55–56.

5. John Durkee to Alexander Copley, May 14, 1829, Copley Family Papers, Bentley Historical Library, University of Michigan, Ann Arbor; Mary Hovey to Martha White, March 15, 1832, Folder 3, L75, Edmund O. Hovey Papers, Indiana State Library, Indianapolis; Bond, *The Civilization of the Old Northwest*, 2–3; Kim M. Gruenwald, *River of Enterprise: The Commercial Origins of Regional Identity in the Ohio Valley, 1790–1850* (Bloomington: Indiana University Press, 2002).

6. Theodore Lloyd Benson, "Planters and Hoosiers: The Development of Sectional Society in Antebellum Indiana and Mississippi" (Ph.D. diss., University of Virginia, 1990). On the Northwest Ordinance of 1787, see Peter S. Onuf, *Statehood and Union: A History of the Northwest Ordinance* (Bloomington: Indiana University Press, 1987). Slavery, as is increasingly well known, existed within the Northwest Territory and the states of the Old Northwest in limited form, especially along the Ohio River. See, for example, James Simeone, *Democracy and Slavery in Frontier Illinois: The Bottomland Republic* (DeKalb: Northern Illinois University Press, 2000). Because the Ohio River itself was not part of the Old Northwest states, in some instances enslaved people were housed on islands in the river, though their daily work took place on the northern shore.

7. Stanley Elkins and Eric McKitrick, "A Meaning for Turner's Frontier. Part I: Democracy in the Old Northwest," *Political Science Quarterly* 69 (1954): 321–353; Francis P. Weisenburger, "The Urbanization of the Middle West: Town and Village in the Pioneer Period," *Indiana Magazine of History* 41 (1945): 19–30; Buley, *The Old Northwest*, 2:147–148.

8. Philander Chase to Sophia Chase, April 18, 1826 (emphasis original), Philander Chase Papers, Special Collections, Kenyon College, Gambier, Ohio; Philander Chase to Bishop [?], April 26, 1825, Chase Papers; Philander Chase to Messrs. Smith & Jenkins, April 25, 1825, Chase Papers. For the classic description of this booster spirit in the West, see Daniel J. Boorstin, *The Americans: The National Experience* (New York: Vintage Books, 1965), 113–168.

9. On optimism and progress in the nineteenth century, see Arthur A. Ekirch, Jr.,

The Idea of Progress in America, 1815–1860 (New York: Peter Smith, 1944; reprint, New York: Columbia University Press, 1951); Robert Nisbet, *History of the Idea of Progress* (New York: Basic Books, Inc., 1980); Stow Persons, "The Cyclical Theory of History in Eighteenth Century America," *American Quarterly* 6 (1954): 147–163; and Timothy L. Smith, "Uncommon Schools: Christian Colleges and Social Idealism in Midwestern America, 1820–1950," in *Indiana Historical Society Lectures, 1976–1977: The History of Education in the Middle West* (Indianapolis: Indiana Historical Society, 1978), 24–26.

10. Esther R. Shipherd, "A Sketch of the Life and Labours of John J. Shipherd," Box 1, John J. Shipherd Papers, Archives, Oberlin College, Oberlin, Ohio, 1–34; Robert S. Fletcher, *A History of Oberlin College: From Its Foundation Through the Civil War*, 2 vols. (Oberlin, OH: Oberlin College, 1943), 1:85–90; the 5,000 acres are noted in "Oberlin Collegiate Institute," *Boston Recorder*, August 14, 1833 (typescript copy in John J. Shipherd Papers, Archives, Oberlin College). John J. Shipherd to L. R. Shipherd, May 24, 1836, John J. Shipherd Papers, Oberlin; John J. Shipherd to Fayette Shipherd, April 11, 1836, John J. Shipherd Papers, Oberlin; Eliza Branch to Fayette Shipherd, May 13, 1836, John J. Shipherd Papers, Oberlin (emphases original).

11. For further explanation of Shipherd's connection to LaGrange and Olivet, see Kenneth H. Wheeler, "The Antebellum College in the Old Northwest: Higher Education and the Defining of the Midwest" (Ph.D. diss., Ohio State University, 1999), 85–88. On Olivet College, see "Early History of Olivet College," *Michigan Historical Collections* 3 (1879–1880): 408–414.

12. Ohio legislators chartered Cincinnati College in 1819, but by 1825, collegiate instruction ended, and a preparatory school attached to the college closed two years later. From then on, a medical school and law school used the Cincinnati College name at times, and from 1836 until 1839 Cincinnati College again had a collegiate department. After 1839 this department also suspended instruction until the late nineteenth century. A historian of the University of Cincinnati has summed up these years as filled with "constant discord, confusion, and disorganization." Reginald C. McGrane, *The University of Cincinnati: A Success Story in Urban Higher Education* (New York: Harper & Row, 1963), 5–45 (quotation, 44). In 1836, Cincinnatians tried again to found a college when the Episcopalian Benjamin P. Aydelott became president of the Woodward High School and expanded the facility into Woodward College. The college operated successfully for a time, but by 1845 was becoming once again simply a fine high school. When Aydelott left the presidency in 1845, the uncle of a replacement candidate informed him that he would have to teach six hours each day and "teach low branches if needed as well as high, for the greater part of the students are boys." Educators abandoned the college department completely in 1851. M. Simpson to Matthew Simpson, July 31, 1845, DC71, Folder 1, Matthew Simpson Papers, Archives, DePauw University, Greencastle, Indiana. See also, on Woodward College, "'Old Woodward': A Memorial Relating to Woodward High School, 1831–1836, & Woodward College, 1836–1851, in the City of Cincinnati" (Cincinnati Historical Society). Not located directly in the city, Lane Seminary existed outside Cincinnati from the 1830s onward; Farmers' College flourished for a time in the late 1840s and early 1850s. The Athenaeum, a precursor of Xavier University, operated in Cincinnati, but the evidence indicates that the Catholic school offered a preparatory education to boys. Francis Joseph Miller, "A History of the Athenaeum of Ohio, 1829–1960" (Ed.D. diss., University of Cincinnati, 1964).

Detroit did have a short-lived Catholic school in the 1840s that may have done some collegiate-level instruction. Charles R. Starring and James O. Knauss, *The Michigan Search for Educational Standards* (Lansing: Michigan Historical Commission, 1968), 1. Also, see the appendices in Colin B. Burke, *American Collegiate Populations: A Test of the Traditional View* (New York: New York University Press, 1982).

13. "The Catalogue of the Officers and Students of Franklin College, New Athens, Ohio; 1848" (St. Clairsville, OH: William Brown, 1848), 16; "Catalogue of the Officers & Students of the Michigan Central College, at Spring Arbor, for the year ending January 1852" (Detroit: Duncklee, Wales & Co., 1852), 22.

14. For a more extended description of denominational motivations for founding colleges, see Vernon Franklin Schwalm, "The Historical Development of the Denominational Colleges in the Old Northwest to 1870" (Ph.D. diss., University of Chicago, 1926), 23–35. See also Smith, "Uncommon Schools."

15. S. W. Williams, "The Ohio Wesleyan University," *National Repository* 1 (June 1877): 486–487. On the hotel and its demise, see Henry Clyde Hubbart, *Ohio Wesleyan's First Hundred Years* (Delaware, OH: Ohio Wesleyan University, 1943), 7–9.

16. Samuel W. Williams, *Pictures of Early Methodism in Ohio* (Cincinnati: Jennings and Graham; New York: Eaton and Mains, 1909), 234–236. The census of 1840 counted 893 Delaware residents. E. T. Nelson, *Fifty Years of the History of the Ohio Wesleyan University, 1844–1894* (Cleveland: Cleveland Printing and Publishing Company, 1895), 12.

17. Hubbart, *Ohio Wesleyan's First Hundred Years*, 9–16; on the eventual demise of Augusta College, see Kenneth H. Wheeler, "Higher Education in the Antebellum Ohio Valley: Slavery, Sectionalism, and the Erosion of Regional Identity," *Ohio Valley History* 8 (Spring 2008): 8–12.

18. Edward Thomson, "Inaugural Address, Delivered at the Ohio Wesleyan University, Delaware, Ohio, at its Annual Commencement, Aug. 6, 1846" (Cincinnati: R. P. Thompson, 1846), 5–6 (emphasis in original).

19. Ibid., 6–7.

20. Ibid., 7–10.

21. George L. Taylor, quoted in Edward Thomson, *Life of Edward Thomson* (Cincinnati: Cranston & Stowe; New York: Phillips & Hunt, 1885), 73. See also Hubbart, *Ohio Wesleyan's First Hundred Years*, 309–310.

22. Report of President Bashford to the Board of Trustees, June 1894, quoted in Nelson, *Fifty Years*, 141. See also Isaac Crook, *The Great Five: The First Faculty of the Ohio Wesleyan University* (Cincinnati: Jennings and Graham; New York: Eaton and Mains, 1908), 50.

23. Williams, *Pictures of Early Methodism*, 288–290. See also *Memorial Record of the Counties of Delaware, Union and Morrow* (Chicago: Lewis Publishing Company, 1895), 14–15.

24. William G. Williams, "The Ohio Wesleyan University, 1844–1894," 21, in Nelson, *Fifty Years*; Williams quoted in Hubbart, *Ohio Wesleyan's First Hundred Years*, 23; also, on rooming and boarding, see Williams, *Pictures of Early Methodism*, 240–242; "Catalogue of the Officers and Students of the Ohio Wesleyan University, for the Academical Year 1844-5. Delaware, Ohio" (Columbus: S. Medary, 1845), 17; Williams, *Pictures of Early Methodism*, 249.

25. [S. J. & M. Strealy?] to Rev. A. McHarry?, 1856? Early OWU Letters, Ohio

Wesleyan Historical Collections, Ohio Wesleyan University, Delaware, Ohio; for population figures, see *History of Delaware County and Ohio* (Chicago: O.L. Baskin & Co., 1880), 337.

26. Mention of the Teacher's Institute, along with a list of the speakers, comes from the Samuel Williams and Samuel Wesley Williams Papers, MSS 148, Ohio Historical Society, Columbus, Ohio; Dr. R. Hills, quoted in "Historical Sketch of the Ohio Wesleyan Female College, Delaware, Ohio," *Historical Sketches of the Higher Educational Institutions, and also of Benevolent and Reformatory Institutions of the State of Ohio* (Columbus, OH: Ohio Commissioner of Common Schools, 1876), unpaginated. See also William G. Williams, "The Ohio Wesleyan University, 1844–1894," 49, in Nelson, *Fifty Years of History*.

27. *History of Delaware County and Ohio*, 254 (quotation), 345.

28. On Kossuth's visit to Delaware, see Ronald K. Huth, "Louis Kossuth in Ohio," *Northwest Ohio Quarterly* 40 (1968): 113; and Samuel W. Williams to Samuel Williams, February 5, 1852, Box 8, Folder 5, MSS 148, Samuel Williams and Samuel Wesley Williams Papers, Ohio Historical Society. McGuffey's visit mentioned in "Catalogue of the Zetagathean Society of the Ohio Wesleyan University, Delaware, Ohio, 1845–'52" (Columbus: Scott & Bascom, 1852), 6; on lecturers at Ohio Wesleyan, see David Mead, *Yankee Eloquence in the Middle West: The Ohio Lyceum, 1850–1870* (East Lansing: Michigan State College Press, 1951), 121, 171–172, 261, 262, 266.

29. Smith, "Uncommon Schools," 3; Mead, *Yankee Eloquence*, 261, 266; Allen Missionary Lyceum, Constitution and By-Laws, VFM 223, Ohio Historical Society, Columbus.

30. *History of Delaware County and Ohio*, 361; *Memorial Record*, 16; Nelson, *Fifty Years*, 97–98, 278, 287; "The Ohio Wesleyan University, Delaware, Ohio," [12] in *Historical Sketches*.

31. Peter G. Mode, *The Frontier Spirit in American Christianity* (New York: The Macmillan Company, 1923), 72–76. For a specific example, see "Western Colleges; a Baccalaureate Address, Delivered July 22, 1847, by Rev. Charles White, D.D., President of Wabash College" (New York: C. W. Benedict, 1848), esp. 31–32.

32. "Address to the Legislature of Ohio," in Philander Chase, "The Star in the West, or Kenyon College, in the Year of our Lord, 1828," 2 (emphasis original) (Columbus: n.p., 1828). The Ohio legislature did support Chase's efforts, although the United States never granted Chase any aid. See also George Franklin Smythe, *Kenyon College: Its First Century* (New Haven: Yale University Press, 1924), 75–78.

33. Chase, "Address to the Legislature of Ohio," 2–3 (emphasis original).

34. Timothy L. Smith, "The Ohio Valley: Testing Ground for America's Experiment in Religious Pluralism," *Church History* 60 (1991): 461–479; Alice Felt Tyler, *Freedom's Ferment: Phases of American Social History from the Colonial Period to the Outbreak of the Civil War* (New York: Harper & Brothers, 1944).

35. Albea Godbold, *The Church College of the Old South* (Durham, NC: Duke University Press, 1944), 147–184, esp. 165, 169. On South Carolina, see Daniel Walker Hollis, *South Carolina College*, vol. 1, *University of South Carolina* (Columbia: University of South Carolina Press, 1951), 172–173.

36. Thomas W. King to Mrs. Edward [Sarah Worthington] King, June 3, [1833?], Box 2, Folder 1, MSS 40, King Family Papers, Ohio Historical Society, Columbus, Ohio. On Presbyterian control of Ohio and Miami Universities, for example, see

"Report of the Ohio Conference on Education," *Wesleyan Christian Advocate* (Cincinnati), October 18, 1842; and, on this point and more generally, Jurgen Herbst, "The Development of Public Universities in the Old Northwest," 97–117, esp. 102–103, in Frederick D. Williams, ed. *The Northwest Ordinance: Essays on Its Formulation, Provisions, and Legacy* (East Lansing: Michigan State University Press, 1989).

37. Summaries of these charters are available for Illinois and Ohio. See Hallie J. Hamilton, "The Role of the Weekly Press in the Proliferation of Colleges in Illinois, 1830–1860" (Ed.D. diss., Indiana University, 1968), 177–200; and Edward A. Miller, "The History of Educational Legislation in Ohio from 1803 to 1850," *Ohio Archaeological and Historical Quarterly* 27 (January-April 1918): 117–118. The anti-Oberlin effort is described in Clayton S. Ellsworth, "Ohio's Legislative Attack upon Abolition Schools," *Mississippi Valley Historical Review* 21 (1934): 379–386.

38. Smith, "Uncommon Schools," esp. 3–40; D. Randall Gabrielse, "Diversity in Church-Associated Colleges in Michigan and Ohio, 1825–1867" (M.A. thesis, Michigan State University, 1993).

Smith and Gabrielse recognized that they were countering long-standing ideas that New Englanders were most responsible for Western colleges. Smith noted the influence on historians of education of Lois Kimball Mathews, *The Expansion of New England: The Spread of New England Settlement and Institutions to the Mississippi River, 1620–1865* (1909; reprint, New York: Russell & Russell, 1962), 171–272, esp. 192, 204–205, 218–219, 232–234, 243, 256, 261–262. See Smith, *Uncommon Schools*, 6–7. Gabrielse found that 33 of 90 professors he studied at Michigan and Ohio schools were natives of New England. 51 of 156 Western professors in his sample graduated from New England colleges.

39. "The First Report of the Society for the Promotion of College and Theological Education at the West" (New York: J. F. Trow & Co., 1844), 6–7. See also Daniel T. Johnson, "Financing the Western Colleges, 1844–1862," *Journal of the Illinois State Historical Society* 65 (1972): 43–54; Harvey Rader Bostrom, "Contributions to Higher Education by the Society for the Promotion of Collegiate and Theological Education at the West, 1843–1874" (Ph.D. diss., New York University, 1960); Charles E. Peterson, Jr., "Theron Baldwin and Higher Education in the Old Northwest" (Ph.D. diss., Johns Hopkins University, 1960); and Daniel T. Johnson, "Puritan Power in Illinois Higher Education Prior to 1870" (Ph.D. diss., University of Wisconsin, 1974). More generally, on finances and the colleges, see James Findlay, "Agency, Denominations and the Western Colleges, 1830–1860: Some Connections between Evangelicalism and American Higher Education," *Church History* 50 (1981): 64–80.

40. "The Fourth Report of the Society for the Promotion of Collegiate and Theological Education at the West" (New York: Leavitt, Trow and Company, 1847), 34; "The First Report . . .," 10, 9 (emphasis original). On the difficulty New Englanders had with accepting the lack of an established religion in the West, see Travis Keene Hedrick, Jr., "Julian Monson Sturtevant and the Moral Machinery of Society: The New England Struggle Against Pluralism in the Old Northwest, 1829–1877" (Ph.D. diss., Brown University, 1974).

41. "The Second Report of the Society for the Promotion of Collegiate and Theological Education at the West" (New York: J. F. Trow & Co., 1845), 15; "Proceedings of a Public meeting in Behalf of the Society for the Promotion of Collegiate and Theological Education at the West," 8–9, in *Permanent Documents of the Society for the*

Promotion of Collegiate and Theological Education at the West, vol. 1 (New York: John F. Trow, 1844–1851).

42. Willis Dunbar, "Public versus Private Control of Higher Education in Michigan, 1817–1855," *Mississippi Valley Historical Review* 22 (1935): 388–391; see also Willis F. Dunbar, *The Michigan Record in Higher Education* (Detroit: Wayne State University Press, 1963), 47–81; and William C. Ringenberg, "The Protestant College on the Michigan Frontier" (Ph.D. diss., Michigan State University, 1970).

2 / Manual Labor and the Producers

1. Typescript of Jonathan Going, "The Inaugural Address at the Anniversary of the Granville Literary & Theological Institution, August 8, 1838," Archives, Denison University, Granville, Ohio. Other examples of the use of "mental, moral, and physical" include "[Ohio] State Commissioner's Report of Common Schools," *Cincinnatus* 3 (1858): 175; and Henry Garst, *Otterbein University, 1847–1907* (Dayton, OH: United Brethren Publishing House, 1907), 123.

2. Charles Alpheus Bennett, *History of Manual and Industrial Education up to 1870* (Peoria, IL: The Manual Arts Press, 1926), 106–156, describes the educational philosophies of Pestalozzi and Fellenberg. On the distinctively American nature of the manual labor system, see Laura Graham, "From Patriarchy to Paternalism: Disestablished Clergymen and the Manual Labor School Movement in Antebellum America" (Ph.D. diss., University of Rochester, 1993), 195–196, ff.13. See also William Alfred Millis, *The History of Hanover College From 1827 to 1927* (Hanover, IN: Hanover College, 1927), 144.

3. Paul Goodman, "The Manual Labor Movement and the Origins of Abolitionism," *Journal of the Early Republic* 13 (1993): 355–388, 360–361 (quotations). Graham, "From Patriarchy to Paternalism," 262, notes that contemporaries recognized that manual labor and abolitionism went hand in hand.

4. A good brief overview of the rise and fall of collegiate manual labor is Frederick C. Waite, "Manual Labor, an Experiment in American Colleges of the Early Nineteenth Century," *Association of American Colleges Bulletin* 36 (1950): 391–400.

5. Theodore D. Weld, *First Annual Report of the Society for Promoting Manual Labor in Literary Institutions* (New York: S. W. Benedict, 1833), 14, 20, 27, 33, 39, 41, 53, 58, 59, 63, 64 (emphasis original).

6. Quoted in Robert S. Fletcher, *A History of Oberlin College: From Its Foundation Through the Civil War*, 2 vols. (Oberlin, OH: Oberlin College, 1943), 2:634.

7. Delazon Smith, *A History of Oberlin, Or New Lights of the West* (Cleveland: S. Underhill & Son, 1837), 15.

8. Fletcher, *History of Oberlin College*, 2:634–645; Lori D. Ginzberg, "The 'Joint Education of the Sexes': Oberlin's Original Vision," in Carol Lasser, ed. *Educating Men and Women Together: Coeducation in a Changing World* (Urbana: University of Illinois Press, 1987), 71.

9. Fletcher, *History of Oberlin College*, 2:646–648, 2:647 (quotation).

10. On Western dedication to manual labor programs, see, for example, Richard S. Taylor, "Western Colleges as 'Securities of Intelligence & Virtue': The Towne-Eddy Report of 1846," *The Old Northwest* 7 (1981): 45; Millis, *The History of Hanover College*, 145–147.

11. Fletcher, *History of Oberlin College*, 2:647–663.

12. Melvin I. Urofsky, "Reforms and Response: The Yale Report of 1828," *History of Education Quarterly* 5 (1965): 53–57. On deviations from the classical curriculum in Indiana and Illinois, see Timothy L. Smith, "Uncommon Schools: Christian Colleges and Social Idealism in Midwestern America, 1820–1950," in *Indiana Historical Society Lectures, 1976–1977: The History of Education in the Middle West* (Indianapolis: Indiana Historical Society, 1978), 11–13, 15–20, 32–36. The standard work on American collegiate curriculum is Frederick Rudolph, *Curriculum: A History of the American Undergraduate Course of Study since 1636* (San Francisco: Jossey-Bass Publishers, 1977).

13. The Yale Report of 1828 is included in Richard Hofstadter and Wilson Smith, eds. *American Higher Education: A Documentary History.* 2 vols. (Chicago: University of Chicago Press, 1961), 1:275–291, 277–279 (quotations, emphasis original).

14. Hofstadter and Smith, *American Higher Education,* 1:283.

15. Urofsky, "Reforms and Response," 61–65; Ralph Eugene Reed, Jr., "Fortresses of Faith: Design and Experience at Southern Evangelical Colleges, 1830–1900" (Ph.D. diss., Emory University, 1991), 195–199. On the Southern attachment to ancient Greeks, see Vernon Louis Parrington, *Main Currents in American Thought: The Romantic Revolution in America, 1800–1860,* vol. 2 (New York: Harcourt, Brace & World, 1927), esp. 73–78, 94–103. On the importance of Greek and Latin and the classical curriculum to Southern male elites, see Wayne K. Durrill, "The Power of Ancient Words: Classical Teaching and Social Change at South Carolina College, 1804–1860," *Journal of Southern History* 65 (1999): 469–498.

16. M. Fairfield to John Pratt, September 19, 1836, 3D1, Office Files, Denison University Archives, Granville, Ohio. Fairfield's 1836 letter does not indicate M.'s full first name, nor the age of Edmund. For this information, see "Lives of the Founders and Builders of Hillsdale College," *The Advance* (Hillsdale, Michigan), June 9, 1886, and the obituary of Edmund Fairfield in *The Oberlin News,* November 25, 1904.

17. Micaiah Fairfield to C. G. Finney, May 23, 1840, Roll 7, Frame 216, Letters Received by Oberlin College, 1822–1866, Archives, Oberlin College.

18. Quoted in Vivian Lyon Moore, *The First Hundred Years of Hillsdale College* (Ann Arbor, MI: Ann Arbor Press, 1943), 15.

19. Charles [Paist?] to C. G. Finney, May 9, 1846, Roll 10, Frame 500, Letters Received by Oberlin College, 1822–1866, Archives, Oberlin College; Sophia C. Noel to J. F. Crowe, December 5, 1849, Box 11, John Finley Crowe Papers, Archives, Hanover College; James Crawford to J. F. Crowe, August 27, 1854, Box 11, John Finley Crowe Papers, Archives, Hanover College.

20. Franklin Merrill to Asa Mahan, June 17, 1837, Roll 4, Frames 294–295, Letters Received by Oberlin College, 1822–1866, Archives, Oberlin College (emphasis original); Jared Baldwin to The Principal of Oberlin College, February 21, 1846, Roll 10, Frames 379–380, Letters Received by Oberlin College, 1822–1866, Archives, Oberlin College.

21. Sarah Worthington King to Edward King, August 30, [1833?], Folder 3, Box 1, King Family Papers, MSS 40, Ohio Historical Society, Columbus, Ohio; Diary of Elijah Evan Edwards, quoted in "Memorabilia of an Earlier Student," *DePauw Alumnus* (November 1958): 8; typescript of Edmund O. Hovey Papers, L75, Indiana State Library, Indianapolis, Indiana; Edmund O. Hovey to Charles White, May 5, 1841,

Folder 2, Edmund O. Hovey Papers, L75, Indiana State Library, Indianapolis, Indiana (emphasis original).

22. Charles B. Storrs, "An Address, Delivered at the Western Reserve College, Hudson, Ohio, February 9, 1831" (Boston: Peirce and Parker, 1831), 12–13 (emphasis original); J. Finley Crowe, "History of Hanover College" (microfilmed typescript copied from manuscript loaned to Indiana State Library), Indiana University, Bloomington. Western advocates of manual labor scorned "the irregular and capricious exercises of the gymnasium." Millis, *History of Hanover College*, 146.

23. Helen Dunn Gates, *A Consecrated Life: A Sketch of the Life and Labors of Rev. Ransom Dunn, D.D. 1818–1900* (Boston: Morning Star Publishing House, 1901), 105; Turner quoted in Smith, "Uncommon Schools" 34–35.

24. Charles Larrabee to John Pratt, April 10, 1834, Folder 2, Container 2, John Stevens Papers, MSS 1455, Western Reserve Historical Society, Cleveland, Ohio; Charles Larrabee to John Pratt, January 5, 1835, Folder 3, Container 2, John Stevens Papers, MSS 1455, Western Reserve Historical Society. See also, on masculinity and manual labor, Graham, "From Patriarchy to Paternalism."

25. Horace Mann, "Demands of the Age on Colleges: Speech Delivered by the Hon. Horace Mann, President of Antioch College, Before the Christian Convention, at its Quadrennial Session, Held at Cincinnati, Ohio, October 5, 1854" (New York: Fowler & Wells, 1857), 22–23 (emphasis original); David F. Allmendinger, Jr., *Paupers and Scholars: The Transformation of Student Life in Nineteenth-Century New England* (New York: St. Martin's Press, 1975), 94; Henry S. Wheaton to Asa Mahan, June 5, 1838, Roll 5, Frames 266–267, Letters Received by Oberlin College, 1822–1866, Archives, Oberlin College.

26. Graham, "From Patriarchy to Paternalism," 174–176, emphasizes the class dimensions that separated gymnastics (upper class) from manual labor (middle class); Philip Alexander Bruce, *History of the University of Virginia, 1819–1919*, 5 vols. (New York: The Macmillan Company, 1920), 2:337–339, 3:153; James Edward Scanlon, *Randolph-Macon College: A Southern History, 1825–1967* (Charlottesville: University Press of Virginia, 1983), lithograph reproduced opposite the title page, and located in the archives of the college; John M. Daley, *Georgetown University: Origin and Early Years* (Washington, DC: Georgetown University Press, 1957), 245–246; Joseph T. Durkin, *Georgetown University: The Middle Years (1840–1900)* (Washington, DC: Georgetown University Press, 1963), 21–22; Robert Emmett Curran, *The Bicentennial History of Georgetown University: From Academy to University, 1789–1889* (Washington, DC: Georgetown University Press, 1993), 173–175. The College of Charleston in South Carolina had gymnastics. J. H. Easterby, *A History of the College of Charleston, Founded 1770* (n.p.: Scribner Press, 1935), 83, 139–140; Thomas Jefferson Wertenbaker, *Princeton, 1746–1896* (Princeton, NJ: Princeton University Press, 1946), 278; Brooks Mather Kelley, *Yale: A History* (New Haven: Yale University Press, 1974), 213; Wilder Dwight Quint, *The Story of Dartmouth* (Boston: Little, Brown, and Company, 1914), 247; David M. Stameshkin, *The Town's College: Middlebury College, 1800–1915* (Middlebury, VT: Middlebury College Press, 1985), 171; Louis C. Hatch, *The History of Bowdoin College* (Portland, ME: Loring, Short & Harmon, 1927), 344–345.

27. William Gardiner Hammond, *Remembrance of Amherst: An Undergraduate's Diary, 1846–1848*, George F. Whicher, ed. (New York: Columbia University Press, 1946), 25, 27, 36, 199.

28. Willis G. Clark, *History of Education in Alabama, 1702–1889* (Washington, DC: Government Printing Office, 1889), 172–173; Colyer Meriwether, *History of Higher Education in South Carolina* (Washington, DC: Government Printing Office, 1889), 95–96; Robert Norman Daniel, *Furman University: A History* (Greenville, SC: Furman University, 1951), 49; Reuben E. Alley, *History of the University of Richmond, 1830–1971* (Charlottesville: University Press of Virginia, 1977), 14–36.

29. James Insley Osborne and Theodore Gregory Gronert, *Wabash College: The First Hundred Years, 1832–1932* (Crawfordsville, IN: R. E. Banta, 1932), 33; Henry Morton Bullock, *A History of Emory University* (Nashville, TN: Parthenon Press, 1936), 45, 53, 67, 81; Allen P. Tankersley, *College Life at Old Oglethorpe* (Athens: University of Georgia Press, 1951), 4–5; Spright Dowell, *A History of Mercer University, 1833–1953* (Macon, GA: Mercer University, 1958), 42–43, 61–62, 75–76, 84; George Washington Paschal, *History of Wake Forest College* (Wake Forest, NC: Wake Forest College, 1935), 1:65–91; *Baptist Weekly Journal*, November 16, 1832, quoted in Carl B. Wilson, "The Baptist Manual Labor School Movement in the United States," *The Baylor Bulletin* 40 (December 1937): 101; Alvin Fayette Lewis, *History of Higher Education in Kentucky* (Washington, DC: Government Printing Office, 1899), 323–324; Mary D. Beaty, *A History of Davidson College* (Davidson, NC: Briarpatch Press, 1988), 21–22. While the program was not explicitly a manual labor program, students at St. Mary's College in Kentucky labored one day each week on the college farm from some point in the 1820s until the Jesuits left in 1846. Lewis, *History of Higher Education in Kentucky*, 133–136.

30. George J. Stevenson, *Increase in Excellence: A History of Emory and Henry College* (New York: Appleton-Century-Crofts, 1963), 3–6, 63, 65, 73–75.

31. Robert S. Bailey, "Narrative of a Visit to the Right Rev. Philander Chase, Bishop of Illinois," *The Charleston Gospel Messenger, and Protestant Episcopal Register* 16 (1839): 276.

32. John Lombard and Justin Davis, "The Georgetown College Cadets," in Joseph Durkin, ed. *Swift Potomac's Lovely Daughter: Two Centuries at Georgetown through Students' Eyes* (Washington, DC: Georgetown University Press, 1990), 249; Bruce, *History of the University of Virginia*, 2:116–117; Ollinger Crenshaw, *General Lee's College: The Rise and Growth of Washington and Lee University* (New York: Random House, 1969), 81; Rod Andrew, Jr., *Long Gray Lines: The Southern Military School Tradition, 1839–1915* (Chapel Hill: University of North Carolina Press, 2001), 1–25; Bruce Allardice, "West Points of the Confederacy: Southern Military Schools and the Confederate Army," *Civil War History* 43 (1997): 310–331; Daniel, *Furman University*, 70; E. Merton Coulter, *College Life in the Old South* (Athens: University of Georgia Press, 1928), 43–46. Generally, though her book focuses on military academies and institutes rather than colleges, see Jennifer R. Green, *Military Education and the Emerging Middle Class in the Old South* (New York, NY: Cambridge University Press, 2008).

33. Rod Andrew, Jr., *Long Gray Lines*, 11–15, 13 (quotations); Allen Kelton, "The University of Nashville, 1850–1875" (Ph.D. diss., George Peabody College for Teachers, 1969), 568.

34. John M. Daley, *Georgetown University: Origin and Early Years* (Washington, DC: Georgetown University Press, 1957), 245–246; James B. Sellers, *History of the University of Alabama: Vol. I, 1818–1902* (University, AL: University of Alabama Press, 1953), 133.

35. Quint, *The Story of Dartmouth*, 136; William Arba Ellis, ed. *Norwich University,*

1819–1911: Her History, Her Graduates, Her Roll of Honor. 3 vols. (Montpelier, VT: Capital City Press, 1911), 1:2, 1:13, 1:72, 1:78, 1:119, 1:116–117. See also Dean Paul Baker, "The Partridge Connection: Alden Partridge and Southern Military Education," (Ph.D. diss., University of North Carolina at Chapel Hill, 1986).

36. The only antebellum exceptions I have found are Oberlin College, where students patronized a gymnasium for some months in 1861, and Urbana University of Ohio, where a faculty member built a gymnasium in 1856 and the trustees hired a Kentucky Military Institute graduate to create a military company, complete with uniforms and mandatory daily drill for all boys older than fourteen years. Frank Higgins, "The Will to Survive": Urbana College, 1850–1975 (Urbana, OH: Urbana College, n.d.), 32–33.

37. On the life of Freeman G. Cary, see Freeman G. Cary, "Early Annals—Autobiography," Cincinnati Historical Society.

38. Carl M. Becker, "Freeman Cary and Farmers' College: An Ohio Educator and an Experiment in Nineteenth Century 'Practical' Education," *Bulletin of the Historical and Philosophical Society of Ohio* 21 (July 1963): 154–157.

39. [Freeman G. Cary], "Difficulties and Discouragements in the Establishment of Institutions for the Promotion of Scientific Agriculture—Plan to be Pursued," *Cincinnatus* 1 (1856): 168; [Freeman G. Cary], "Agricultural Colleges—Farmers' College," *Cincinnatus* 3 (1858): 83–84; [Cary], "Difficulties and Discouragements," 169–170 (quotations); J. R. Williams, "Address on Agricultural Education: Delivered at the State Fair, Syracuse, N.Y., October 8, 1858," *Cincinnatus* 3 (1858): 530–556, esp. 544.

40. [Freeman G. Cary], "Our College, Errors in respect to Its Object and Aim," *Cincinnatus* 2 (1857): 241, 248; F. G. Cary, "Dedication of Polytechnic Hall," *Cincinnatus* 1 (1856): 543.

41. [Freeman G. Cary], "Institutions for the Promotion of Scientific Agriculture—Proposed Advantages", *Cincinnatus* 1 (1856): 289.

42. Henry W. Ward, *Western-Leander-Clark College, 1856–1911* (Dayton, OH: Otterbein Press, 1911), 51 (emphasis original). Work-study programs would never entirely disappear. In the postbellum United States they were most prominent in Appalachia, evidenced by schools such as Berea in Kentucky, Warren Wilson in North Carolina, and Berry in Georgia.

43. Roger L. Geiger, "The Rise and Fall of Useful Knowledge: Higher Education for Science, Agriculture, and the Mechanic Arts, 1850–1875," 153–168, in Roger Geiger, ed. *The American College in the Nineteenth Century* (Nashville, TN: Vanderbilt University Press, 2000). See also Earle D. Ross, "The Manual Labor Experiment in the Land Grant College," *Mississippi Valley Historical Review* 21 (1935): 513–528.

44. Samuel Miller to Robert H. Bishop, September 27, 1847, Bishop Manuscripts Collection, Miami University, Oxford, Ohio, quoted in Becker, "Freeman Cary and Farmers' College," 159. Generally, on Farmers' College, see also Becker, "The Patriarch of Farmers' College," *Bulletin of the Cincinnati Historical Society* 23 (1965): 104–118; and A. B. Huston, *Historical Sketch of Farmers' College* (n.p.: Students' Association of Farmers' College, n.d.).

45. Flint quoted in James Shortridge, *The Middle West: Its Meaning in American Culture* (Lawrence: University Press of Kansas, 1989), 14; Lewis Clarke to Oliver Clarke, August 1, 1840, Folder 1840–1841, Correspondence, Stevens mss II, Lilly

Library, Indiana University, Bloomington, Indiana; Gayle Thornbrough, ed. *The Diary of Calvin Fletcher,* 9 vols. (Indianapolis: Indiana Historical Society, 1972–1983), 1:89; William E. and Ophia D. Smith, eds. "The Diary of Charles Peabody," *Bulletin of the Historical and Philosophical Society of Ohio* 11 (1953): 286; John Meyer to Henry Wolf, July 8, 1848, Folder 6, Box 1, Series 2, Oberlin File, Archives, Oberlin College, Oberlin, Ohio. These ideas are buttressed by James E. Davis, "'New Aspects of Men and New Forms of Society': The Old Northwest, 1790–1820," *Journal of the Illinois State Historical Society* 69 (1976): 164–172.

3 / Coeducation and Usefulness

1. J. H. Fairchild, *Oberlin. Its Origin, Progress and Results* (Oberlin: R. Butler, 1871), 65–66.

2. *Circular,* March 1834, quoted in Robert S. Fletcher, *A History of Oberlin College: From Its Foundation Through the Civil War,* 2 vols. (Oberlin, OH: Oberlin College, 1943), 1: 373; Lori D. Ginzberg, "The 'Joint Education of the Sexes': Oberlin's Original Vision," in Carol Lasser, ed. *Educating Men and Women Together: Coeducation in a Changing World* (Urbana: University of Illinois Press, 1987), 67–80; Ronald W. Hogeland, "Coeducation of the Sexes at Oberlin College: A Study of Social Ideas in Mid-Nineteenth-Century America," *Journal of Social History* 6 (1972–1973): 160–176; Fletcher, *History of Oberlin College, passim.*

3. Ginzberg, "The 'Joint Education of the Sexes,'" 71; Fletcher, *History of Oberlin College,* 1: 376, 379–380.

Historians have never adequately delineated the contours and chronology of coeducation. The best efforts are Thomas Woody, *A History of Women's Education in the United States,* 2 vols. (1929; reprint, New York: Octagon Books, 1966); and Barbara Miller Solomon, *In the Company of Educated Women: A History of Women and Higher Education in America* (New Haven: Yale University Press, 1985).

Some studies of early collegiate coeducation have focused on the lack of perfect equality at these schools. See, for example, John Rury and Glenn Harper, "The Trouble with Coeducation: Mann and Women at Antioch, 1853–1860," *History of Education Quarterly* 26 (1986): 481–502. While historians such as Ronald Hogeland, John Rury, and Glenn Harper produced valuable studies, in the 1970s and 1980s, when numerous women's colleges became coeducational or closed their doors completely, some scholars were unpersuasively critical of the origins of collegiate coeducation. In 1974, Jill Conway, president of Smith College, a woman's college, skewered Oberlin leaders for having "strictly economic" considerations when they introduced coeducation, and for considering the improvement of women's minds only as they related to "services they might provide for men." In 1978, Patricia Albjerg Graham repeated this refrain. These ventures were monetarily driven; women were at college to darn men's socks or civilize male students. Jill Conway, "Perspectives on the History of Women's Education in the United States," *History of Education Quarterly* 14 (1974): 6–7; Patricia Albjerg Graham, "Expansion and Exclusion: A History of Women in American Higher Education," *Signs: Journal of Women in Culture and Society* 3 (1978): 764. See also, in this vein, Florence Howe, *Myths of Coeducation: Selected Essays, 1964–1983* (Bloomington: Indiana University Press, 1984), esp. 207–209; and Rosalind Rosenberg, "The Limits of Access: The History of Coeducation in America," in John Mack Faragher and Florence Howe, eds. *Women and Higher Education in American History: Essays From the Mount*

Holyoke College Sesquicentennial Symposia (New York: W. W. Norton & Company, 1988), 107–129, esp. 110–111.

4. Doris Jeanne Malkmus, "Capable Women and Refined Ladies: Two Visions of American Women's Higher Education, 1760–1861" (Ph.D. dissertation, University of Iowa, 2001), 15–25.

5. Malkmus, ibid., 53–94.

6. Ibid.

7. Vivian Lyon Moore, *The First Hundred Years of Hillsdale College* (Ann Arbor, MI: Ann Arbor Press, 1943), 6–20.

8. Generally on the influence of Oberlin, see Robert S. Fletcher, "Oberlin and Co-Education," *Ohio State Archaeological and Historical Quarterly* 47 (1938): 1–19, esp. 8; and Malkmus, "Capable Women and Refined Ladies," 244. A detailed examination of how the Oberlin example influenced Michigan schools comes from William C. Ringenberg, "The Oberlin College Influence in Early Michigan," *The Old Northwest* 3 (1977): 111–131. Susan Rumsey Strong, "'The Most Natural Way in the World': Coeducation at Nineteenth-Century Alfred University" (Ph.D. diss., University of Rochester, 1995), *passim*, esp. 197, 250.

9. Data on when colleges became coeducational comes from Doris Malkmus, "Small Towns, Small Sects, and Coeducation: The Origins of Midwestern Rural Gender" (paper presented to the History of Education Society, Chicago, Illinois, October 30, 1998); and Malkmus, "Capable Women and Refined Ladies," Table 7. See also Doris Malkmus, "Origins of Coeducation in Antebellum Iowa," *The Annals of Iowa* 58 (Spring 1999): 162–196. On Central and Genessee, see Kathryn M. Kerns, "Antebellum Higher Education for Women in Western New York State" (Ph.D. diss., University of Pennsylvania, 1993), esp. 11–12, 20–22, 52–55. Central College, a fascinating school, was not long-lasting, closing by 1861. (The Central College faculty included both a woman and an African-American man. See Carol Lasser and Marlene Merrill, eds. *Soul Mates: The Oberlin Correspondence of Lucy Stone and Antoinette Brown, 1846–1850* [Oberlin, OH: Oberlin College, 1983], 8.) The college catalogues of Genessee in the early 1850s made no mention of females as students in the college. When the catalogue listed female names, only initials appeared before the surname, hiding their sex.

10. G. C. Sellew to Jerusha Sellew, June 12, 1835, in Recent Acquisitions, 1969, Stowe-Day Foundation, Hartford, Connecticut, quoted in Robert H. Abzug, *Passionate Liberator: Theodore Dwight Weld and the Dilemma of Reform* (New York: Oxford University Press, 1980), 76; Strong, "The Most Natural Way," passim. The classic work on the cult of domesticity is Nancy F. Cott, *The Bonds of Womanhood: "Woman's Sphere" in New England, 1780–1835* (New Haven: Yale University Press, 1977).

11. Frank Higgins, *"The Will to Survive": Urbana College, 1850–1975* (Urbana, OH: Urbana College, n.d.), 6–13, 16; Ophia D. Smith, "The New Jerusalem Church in Ohio From 1848 to 1870," *Ohio State Archaeological and Historical Quarterly* 62 (January 1953): 25–54.

12. E. I. F. Williams, *Heidelberg: Democratic Christian College, 1850–1950* (Menasha, WI: George Banta Publishing, 1952), 19, 68, 73, 81, 86–88, 100, 106, 142; George W. Williard, *The History of Heidelberg College . . .* (Cincinnati: Elm Street Printing, 1879), 22, 27, 74, 76, 79–81 (quotation, 80).

13. William Fisk, "The Associate Reformed Church Marches Westward," 48–61 (quotation, 52) in E. B. Welsh, ed. *Buckeye Presbyterianism* (n.p.: n.p., 1968). See also

Ray A. King, *A History of the Associate Reformed Presbyterian Church* (Charlotte, NC: Board of Christian Education of the Associate Reformed Presbyterian Church, 1966), esp. 65–80; Erving E. Beauregard, *Old Franklin, the Eternal Touch: A History of Franklin College, New Athens, Harrison County, Ohio* (Lanham, MD: University Press of America, 1983), gives the Scotch-Irish name statistics in three appendices on pp. 211–212; Paul Gamble, *History of Westminster College, 1852–1977* (New Wilmington, PA: Westminster College, 1977), 6; F. Garvin Davenport, *Monmouth College: The First Hundred Years, 1853–1953* (Cedar Rapids, IA: The Torch Press, 1953), 13–45.

14. Lewis quoted in Henry Garst, *Otterbein University, 1847–1907* (Dayton, OH: United Brethren Publishing House, 1907), 28; Garst, 79–85 (quotation, 79); J. Bruce Behney and Paul H. Eller, *The History of the Evangelical United Brethren Church*, Kenneth W. Krueger, ed. (Nashville, TN.: Abingdon, 1979), 7, 159–160.

15. Catherine A. Brekus, *Strangers and Pilgrims: Female Preaching in America, 1740–1845* (Chapel Hill: University of North Carolina Press, 1998), 7–8; Nathan O. Hatch, *The Democratization of American Christianity* (New Haven: Yale University Press, 1989).

16. M. Simpson to M. Simpson, March 6, 1843, DC71, Folder 6, Matthew Simpson Papers, Archives, Roy O. West Library, DePauw University, Greencastle, Indiana.

17. On the Society of Friends at that time in America, see Thomas D. Hamm, *The Transformation of American Quakerism: Orthodox Friends, 1800–1907* (Bloomington: Indiana University Press, 1988). On Earlham College, see Opal Thornburg, *Earlham: The Story of the College, 1847–1962* (Richmond, IN: Earlham College Press, 1963); and Thomas D. Hamm, *Earlham College: A History, 1847–1997* (Bloomington: Indiana University Press, 1997), 12–13, 50–51. On Quakerism and women, see Elisabeth Anthony Dexter, *Career Women of America, 1776–1840* (Francestown, NH: Marshall Jones Company, 1950), 55–57.

18. William Tallack, *Friendly Sketches in America* (London: A. W. Bennett, 1861), 57 ff., quoted in Thornburg, *Earlham*, 80–81.

19. Norman Allen Baxter, *History of the Freewill Baptists: A Study in New England Separatism* (Rochester, NY: American Baptist Historical Society, 1957), 137, 31; Dexter, *Career Women*, 58–60.

20. Charles Breunig, "The Founding of Lawrence University," *Voyageur: Historical Review of Brown County and Northeast Wisconsin* 9 (1993): 2–14 (quotation, 6).

21. Breunig, ibid., 12–13 (quotation, 12); Malkmus, "Capable Women and Refined Ladies," 253–254 (quotation, 253).

22. S. W. Williams, "The Ohio Wesleyan University," *National Repository* 1 (June 1877): 487.

23. Joseph Frazier Wall, *Grinnell College in the Nineteenth Century: From Salvation to Service* (Ames: Iowa State University Press, 1997), 110–112.

24. Prudden quoted in Fletcher, *History of Oberlin College*, 718; Williams quoted in Higgins, "*The Will to Survive*," 20.

25. Hugh Smart to Professor Pratt, February 5, 1833, Container 2, Folder 2, John Stevens Papers, MSS 1455, Western Reserve Historical Society, Cleveland, Ohio; Aaron Sadner Lindsley to Rev. C. G. Finney, June 6, 1837, Folder "Cowles Papers—undated and 1835–1839," Box 4, Series 3, Robert S. Fletcher Papers, Oberlin College Archives.

26. John Hovey to Lucy M. Bricket, August 27, 1852, VFM 783, Ohio Historical Society, Columbus (emphasis original).

27. Princess A. Miller Autograph Book (unpaginated), Ohio Historical Society, Columbus, Ohio. On usefulness, see also E. Anthony Rotundo, "Body and Soul: Changing Ideals of American Middle-Class Manhood, 1770–1920," *Journal of Social History* 16 (1983): 23–38. Rotundo argues that usefulness, among men, was an extremely common value in the late eighteenth century, but that in the nineteenth century, the value of self-improvement came to the fore among American men. This author finds a great amount of discussion of usefulness through the antebellum period in the West by both women and men. See Kenneth H. Wheeler, "How Colleges Shaped a Public Culture of Usefulness," in Andrew R. L. Cayton and Stuart D. Hobbs, eds. *The Center of a Great Empire: The Ohio Country in the Early American Republic* (Athens: Ohio University Press, 2005), esp. 114–115.

28. Lori D. Ginzberg, "Women in an Evangelical Community: Oberlin, 1835–1850," *Ohio History* 89 (Winter 1980): 78–88, esp. 85–86. See also Lori D. Ginzberg, "The 'Joint Education of the Sexes': Oberlin's Original Vision," in Carol Lasser, ed. *Educating Men and Women Together: Coeducation in a Changing World* (Urbana: University of Illinois Press, 1987), 67–80; and Barbara Miller Solomon, "The Oberlin Model and Its Impact on Other Colleges," in Lasser, ed. *Educating Men and Women Together*, 81–90.

29. Carol Lasser and Marlene Deahl Merrill, eds. *Friends and Sisters: Letters between Lucy Stone and Antoinette Brown Blackwell, 1846–93* (Urbana: University of Illinois Press, 1987), 203.

My interpretation differs greatly from that offered by Mary Kelley in *Learning to Stand and Speak: Women, Education, and Public Life in America's Republic* (Chapel Hill: University of North Carolina Press, 2006). Kelley asserted that single-sex schools were instrumental in leading American women into public life. Kelley acknowledged that most American girls and young women attended coeducational schools, but argued that those females who came from elite families and attended single-sex schools made the greatest contributions to public life. She proceeded to write about single-sex education as though it were the only education available to females. Ironically, she drew her book title from the correspondence of Oberlin graduates Lucy Stone and Antoinette Brown. Kelley twice referred to Stone as a Mount Holyoke graduate though Stone spent only a few months there, years before she enrolled at Oberlin. Kelley, *Learning to Stand and Speak*, esp. 1–2, 32, 39–40, 132, 275, 278–79. On Stone's time at Mount Holyoke, see Lasser and Merrill, *Friends and Sisters*, 6.

30. Heidemarie Z. Weidner, "Coeducation and Jesuit *Ratio Studiorum* in Indiana: Rhetoric and Composition Instruction at 19th-Century Butler and Notre Dame" (Ph.D. diss., University of Louisville, 1991), 122–132, (quotation, 131); Fletcher, *History of Oberlin College*, 1: 293; Lasser and Merrill, eds., *Friends and Sisters*, 43.

31. Gwendolyn B. Willis, ed. and compiler, "Olympia Brown, An Autobiography," *Annual Journal of The Universalist Historical Society* 4 (1963): 1–12; Olympia Brown, *Acquaintances, Old and New, Among Reformers* (Milwaukee: S. E. Tate, 1911), 8–9.

32. Willis, "Olympia Brown," 14–19.

33. Ibid., 18–19.

34. Ibid., 19–21.

35. Ibid., 23–26.

36. Ibid., 27–31.

37. Brown, *Acquaintances*, 55–79; Willis, "Olympia Brown," 31–40 (quotation, 38).

38. Willis, "Olympia Brown," 40–76.

39. Kathryn Kish Sklar, "Ohio 1903: Heartland of Progressive Reform," in Geoffrey Parker, Richard Sisson, and William Russell Coil, eds. *Ohio and the World, 1753–2053: Essays Toward a New History of Ohio* (Columbus: Ohio State University Press, 2005), 95–127 (quotations, 96, 112, 113). On the twentieth-century leadership of Midwestern feminists, see Ruth Rosen, *The World Split Open: How the Modern Women's Movement Changed America* (New York: Penguin, 2000), 4, 69–70, 78, 110, 267–270.

40. Petition to the Board of Trustees, 23 June 1903, Archives, Robert Scott Small Library, College of Charleston, South Carolina, quoted in Amy Thompson McCandless, "Maintaining the Spirit and Tone of Robust Manliness: The Battle Against Coeducation at Southern Colleges and Universities, 1890–1940," *NWSA Journal* 2 (1990): 199–216 (quotation, 201). The literature on Southern honor is vast. Begin with the classic work, Bertram Wyatt-Brown, *Southern Honor: Ethics and Behavior in the Old South* (New York: Oxford University Press, 1982). On reform and feminism, see Dorothy Ann Gay, "The Tangled Skein of Romanticism and Violence in the Old South: The Southern Response to Abolitionism and Feminism, 1830–1861" (Ph.D. diss., University of North Carolina, 1975); Clement Eaton, *Freedom of Thought in the Old South* (Durham, N.C.: Duke University Press, 1940), esp. 315–332. See also W. J. Cash, *The Mind of the South* (New York: Vintage Books, 1941), esp. 90–102. On the educational options available to females, see Christie Anne Farnham, *The Education of the Southern Belle: Higher Education and Student Socialization in the Antebellum South* (New York: New York University Press, 1995).

41. Richard S. Taylor, "Western Colleges as 'Securities of Intelligence & Virtue': The Towne-Eddy Report of 1846," *The Old Northwest* 7 (1981): 41–66 (quotations, 44–45).

42. Alice Hamilton, *Exploring the Dangerous Trades: The Autobiography of Alice Hamilton, M.D.* (Boston: Little, Brown and Company, 1943), 40. On heightened opposition to collegiate coeducation, see Roger L. Geiger, "New Themes in the History of Nineteenth-Century Colleges," in Roger Geiger, ed. *The American College in the Nineteenth Century* (Nashville, TN: Vanderbilt University Press, 2000), 15.

43. Mabel Newcomer, *A Century of Higher Education for American Women* (New York: Harper & Brothers, 1959), 14, lists the first seven coeducational state universities as Iowa, Wisconsin, Kansas, Indiana, Minnesota, Missouri, and Michigan; Solomon, *In the Company*, 53–57. Newcomer, *A Century of Higher Education*, 12, also mentions that the University of Deseret, the forerunner of the University of Utah, which operated only from 1850 to 1851 before closing until after 1865, enrolled women in 1851. Mary Leo Joseph Devine, "A Study of the Historical Development of Coeducation in American Higher Education" (Ph.D. diss., Boston College, 1966), 201, 205, agrees with Newcomer's list, with the addition of the University of Washington, which Devine says admitted women from its opening in 1862; Linda Lehmann Goldstein, "'Without Compromising in Any Particular': The Success of Medical Coeducation in Cleveland, 1850–1856," *Caduceus: A Museum Quarterly for the Health Sciences* 10 (1994): 101–116. The next school with coeducational medical graduates was the University of Michigan, beginning in 1869. On the life of Harper, begin with James P. Wind, *The Bible and the University: The Messianic Vision of William Rainey Harper* (Atlanta: Scholars Press, 1987).

44. P. P. Stewart to Levi Burnell, April 10, 1837, Roll 4, Frame 137, Letters Received by Oberlin College, 1822–1866, Archives, Oberlin College, Oberlin, Ohio.

45. Eliza Dana to Mary B. "Polly" Dana, October 19, 1835, Box 1, Folder 9, MSS 181, Dana Family Papers, Ohio Historical Society, Columbus, Ohio; Mary Hovey to "Mother" [Martha Carter], December 25, 1833, Folder 3, L75, Edmund O. Hovey Papers, Indiana State Library, Indianapolis, Indiana.

46. W. Le Conte Stevens, "University Education for Women," *North American Review* 136 (1883): 30. Generally, see Malkmus, "Capable Women and Refined Ladies," chap. 6.

4 / Students, Piety, and Debate

1. Henry Caswall, *America and the American Church* (1839; reprint: New York: Arno Press and the New York Times, 1969), 34; Robert S. Fletcher, *A History of Oberlin College: From Its Foundation Through the Civil War*, 2 vols. (Oberlin, OH: Oberlin College, 1943), 2: 507; Colin B. Burke, *American Collegiate Populations: A Test of the Traditional View* (New York: New York University Press, 1982), 90–136, esp. 102, 116, 120, 126, 127.

2. Ralph Eugene Reed, Jr., "Fortresses of Faith: Design and Experience at Southern Evangelical Colleges, 1830–1900" (Ph.D. diss., Emory University, 1991), 122.

3. David F. Allmendinger, Jr., *Paupers and Scholars: The Transformation of Student Life in Nineteenth-Century New England* (New York: St. Martin's Press, 1975).

4. Wilson Smith, "Apologia pro Alma Matre: The College as Community in Ante-Bellum America," in Stanley Elkins and Eric McKitrick, eds. *The Hofstadter Aegis: A Memorial* (New York: Alfred A. Knopf, 1974), 125–153.

5. Horace Wellington to Brother and Sister Keys, April 19, 1847, Horace Wellington Letter, Bentley Historical Library, University of Michigan, Ann Arbor, Michigan; Edwin I. Farwell to Timothy H. Ball, December 24, [1847?], M-309, Timothy Horton Ball Papers, Indiana Historical Society, Indianapolis.

6. E. Thomson to Thomas A. Morris, March 3, 1850, Box 1, Morris Papers, Archives, Ohio Wesleyan Historical Collections, Ohio Wesleyan University, Delaware, Ohio; Samuel Williams to Stephen [Widney?], February 9, 1847, copied into "memoirs of Samuel Williams," 5:869, Box 2, Samuel Williams and Samuel Wesley Williams Papers, MSS 148, Ohio Historical Society, Columbus. See also Norman Rovick, "The Impact of Religious Revivalism Upon Five Selected Ohio Colleges of the Mid-Nineteenth Century" (M.A. thesis, Ohio State University, 1965). Rovick examined Western Reserve, Marietta, Oberlin, Granville, and Ohio Wesleyan.

7. Benjamin Harrison to R. H. Bishop, August 28, 1850 and March 11, 1855, Roll 1, Series 1, Benjamin Harrison Papers, Library of Congress (microfilm edition).

8. Elam J. Comings to Asa Mahan, January 26, 1836, Roll 2: September 1834–February 1836, Letters Received by Oberlin College, 1822–1866, Archives, Oberlin College (emphasis original); Franklin Merrill to Asa Mahan, June 17, 1837, Roll 4, Frames 294–295, Letters Received by Oberlin College, 1822–1866, Archives, Oberlin College (emphasis original); Rev. J. Mills to Matthew Simpson, October 18, 1841, Box 4, Bishop Matthew Simpson Papers, Library of Congress (emphasis original).

9. Charles Richard Williams, ed. *Diary and Letters of Rutherford Birchard Hayes: Nineteenth President of the United States* (Columbus, OH: The Ohio State Archaeological and Historical Society, 1922), 1:36–37; Caleb Manchester to A. B. Morse, February 27, 1859, Box 1, Marion Morse Davis Papers, Burton Historical Collection, Detroit Public Library.

10. Thomas S. Harding, *College Literary Societies: Their Contribution to Higher Education in the United States, 1815–1876* (New York: Pageant Press, 1971); James McLachlan, "The *Choice of Hercules*: American Student Societies in the Early 19th Century," in Lawrence Stone, ed. *The University in Society: Europe, Scotland, and the United States from the 16th to the 20th Century,* vol. II (Princeton, NJ: Princeton University Press, 1974), 449–494; Henry D. Sheldon, *Student Life and Customs* (New York: D. Appleton and Company, 1901), 125–142, esp. 133–135 on the decline of collegiate literary and debate societies generally, and their persistence in the Middle West into the twentieth century.

11. Homer Wheeler to Maro Wheeler, July 22, 1846, Folder 2, Container 1, Thomas, Wheeler and White Family Papers, MSS 3412, Western Reserve Historical Society, Cleveland, Ohio; John Dunmore Lang, *Religion and Education in America* (London: Thomas Ward and Co., 1840), 293–294. See also Rita Segel Saslaw, "Student Societies: Nineteenth Century Establishment" (Ph.D. diss., Case Western Reserve University, 1971), 124–125.

12. Journal of the Calliopean Society of Granville Institution, Vol. 1, 1835 (unpaginated), Archives, Denison University.

13. Ibid.

14. Ibid.

15. Lyman C. Draper, future founder of the State Historical Society of Wisconsin, founded the Calliopean Society at Granville and served as corresponding secretary. William B. Hesseltine, *Pioneer's Mission: The Story of Lyman Copeland Draper* (Madison: The State Historical Society of Wisconsin, 1954), 18–23.

16. Journal of the Calliopean Society of Granville Institution, Vol. 1, 1835.

17. Ibid. The context for Granger's actions is provided by William T. Utter, *Granville: The Story of an Ohio Village* (Granville, OH: Granville Historical Society, Denison University, 1956), 166–181.

18. Journal of the Calliopean Society of Granville Institution, Vol. 1, 1835.

19. The Calliopean Society had made an auspicious choice. The following January the state legislature sent Allen to the United States Senate. Francis P. Weisenburger, *The Passing of the Frontier: 1825–1850* (Columbus: Ohio State Archaeological and Historical Society, 1941), 328–330.

20. Manuscript copy of "Autobiography of John Calvin Hanna," SC 645, Illinois State Historical Society, Springfield, Illinois. Generally, on the importance of oratory, including debate, in the culture of the West, see Ralph Leslie Rusk, *The Literature of the Middle Western Frontier,* 2 vols. (New York: Columbia University Press, 1925), 1:204–210.

21. J. Merton England, ed. *Buckeye Schoolmaster: A Chronicle of Midwestern Rural Life, 1853–1865* (Bowling Green, OH: Bowling Green State University Popular Press, 1996), esp. 11–27, 71–74, 99, 147–185. The evidence concerning public debate is extensive. See, for example, Paul H. Boase, "Interdenominational Polemics on the Ohio Frontier," *Bulletin of the Historical and Philosophical Society of Ohio* 20 (1962): 99–100; Bill J. Humble, *Campbell and Controversy: The Debates of Alexander Campbell* (Joplin, MO: College Press, 1986), esp. 78–156; and Earl Irvin West, "Early Cincinnati's 'Unprecedented Spectacle,'" *Ohio History* 79 (Winter 1970): 5–17.

22. M. A. Rumley to Brother Peters, April 12, 1832, Church History—American

Home Missionary Society Mss., L187, Indiana State Library, Indianapolis; Boase, "Interdenominational Polemics," 106–107.

23. W. B. Riggin to Augustus K. Riggin, March 29, 1844, Folder 1, Riggin Family Papers, SC 1272, Illinois State Historical Society, Springfield, Illinois; Samuel Galloway to John A. Trimble, January 12, 1837, Box 1, Folder 3, John A. Trimble Family Papers, MSS 249, Ohio Historical Society, Columbus; A. Bartholomew to J. Bartholomew, January 6, 1841, Bartholomew mss., Lilly Library, Indiana University, Bloomington; Diary of Elijah Evan Edwards, February 8, 1850, Folder 2, L49, Indiana State Library, Indianapolis (emphasis original).

24. Lois Smith Murray, *Baylor at Independence* (Waco, TX: Baylor University Press, 1972), 84, says that no agency was more active than the Masons in maintaining colleges. On Masonic schools, see, for example, "Catalogue of the East Alabama Masonic Female Institute, of Talladega, Alabama" (Montgomery: Advertiser and Gazette Steam Power Press Book Office, 1854); and "Catalogue of the Officers and Students of the Southern Masonic Female College at Covington, Georgia" (Atlanta: C. R. Hanleiter & Co., 1856), which specified that it was "[f]ounded and controlled by the Grand Lodge of the State of Georgia." Colin Burke mentions that other schools, located in Alabama, Tennessee, and Missouri, were Masonic-affiliated. See Burke, *American Collegiate Populations*, 308, 316, 341. Baylor's president joined the Masons. Murray, *Baylor at Independence*, 94. So did one of the presidents of the University of Mississippi, where the Masons laid the cornerstone on every important building on campus until 1912. James Allen Cabaniss, *A History of the University of Mississippi* (University, MS: University of Mississippi, 1949), 6–8, 38–39. See also Allen Kelton, "The University of Nashville, 1850–1875" (Ph.D. diss., George Peabody College for Teachers, 1969), 459–463; J. H. Easterby, *A History of the College of Charleston, Founded 1770* (n.p.: Scribner Press, 1935), 78; David Duncan Wallace, *History of Wofford College, 1854–1949* (Nashville, TN: Vanderbilt University Press, 1951), 43; and Susan H. Godson et al., *The College of William and Mary: A History.* Volume I, 1693–1888 (Williamsburg, VA: King and Queen Press, 1993), 289.

25. Cabaniss, *A History of the University of Mississippi*, 56; James B. Sellers, *History of the University of Alabama: Volume 1, 1818–1902* (University, AL: University of Alabama Press, 1953), 118–120; John William Burgess, "A Civil War Boyhood," *Atlantic*, February–March 1933, quoted in Winstead Paine Bone, *A History of Cumberland University, 1842–1935* (Lebanon, TN: The Author, 1935), 83–85. For other mention of students with slaves, see John D. Wright, Jr., *Transylvania: Tutor to the West* (Lexington: University Press of Kentucky, 1975), 94; Godson et al., *The College of William & Mary*, 186.

26. On Southern college use, employment, and ownership of slaves, see, for example, Sellers, *History of the University of Alabama*, 31, 38–41; Lester B. Shippee, ed. *Bishop Whipple's Southern Diary, 1843–1844*, 60, quoted in Edgar W. Knight, ed. *A Documentary History of Education in the South Before 1860*, 5 vols. (Chapel Hill: University of North Carolina Press, 1953), 4:337.

27. Oran Roberts, quoted in Sellers, *History of the University of Alabama*, 128; Sellers, *History of the University of Alabama*, 233–236; see also, for more accounts of student attacks on slaves, Daniel Walker Hollis, *South Carolina College*, vol. 1, *University of South Carolina* (Columbia: University of South Carolina Press, 1951), 57–58; Philip Alexander Bruce, *History of the University of Virginia, 1818–1919*, 5 vols. (New York:

The Macmillan Company, 1920), 2:291; Cabaniss, *History of the University of Missississippi*, 54; and Robert F. Pace, *Halls of Honor: College Men in the Old South* (Baton Rouge: Louisiana State University Press, 2004), 47–51.

28. Knight, *Documentary History*, 3:91, 95; Sellers, *History of the University of Alabama*, 236; William Sydney Mullins, quoted in Judith Mitchell Ishkanian, "Religion and Honor at Chapel Hill: The College Odyssey of William Sydney Mullins, 1840–1842" (Ph.D. diss., University of California, Santa Barbara, 1993), 153; the "Branham affair" at the University of Mississippi is covered in Cabaniss, *History of the University of Mississippi*, 50–54 (first two quotations on 50); and Knight, *Documentary History*, 3:466–473 (final quotation, made by the chancellor himself, on 470). See also, on students frequenting brothels, Bruce, *History of the University of Virginia*, 2:274.

29. Bliss Perry, ed. *The Heart of Emerson's Journals* (Boston: Houghton Mifflin Company, 1909), 115, quoted in Knight, *Documentary History*, 4:310.

30. Riddelle quoted in Opal Thornburg, *Earlham: The Story of the College, 1847–1962* (Richmond, IN: Earlham College Press, 1963), 113.

31. John S. Brubacher and Willis Rudy, *Higher Education in Transition: A History of American Colleges and Universities, 1636–1968* (1958; revised and enlarged, New York: Harper & Row 1968), 51; Helen Lefkowitz Horowitz, *Campus Life: Undergraduate Cultures From the End of the Eighteenth Century to the Present* (New York: Alfred A. Knopf, 1987), 11. Ishkanian, "Religion and Honor at Chapel Hill," 120–121; Reed, "Fortresses of Faith," 122. The literature on student riots includes Allmendinger, *Paupers and Scholars*, 107–110; Horowitz, *Campus Life*, 24–29; Richard Hofstadter and Walter P. Metzger, *The Development of Academic Freedom in the United States* (New York: Columbia University Press, 1955), esp. 309–311; Reed, "Fortresses of Faith," esp. 121–25; George P. Schmidt, *The Liberal Arts College: A Chapter in American Cultural History* (New Brunswick, NJ: Rutgers University Press, 1957), 81–88; and Stephen T. Schreiber, "American College Student Riots and Disorders Between 1815 and the Civil War" (Ed.D. diss., Indiana University, 1979). Schreiber counted as riots a few disturbances at Ohio University that did not rise to my definition of riots as collective violence resulting in property damage or human injury.

32. J. J. Hopkins, "Old College Days," *The Reunion* (Hillsdale, MI) (July 8, 1885): 158.

33. Thomas Lesick Lawrence, *The Lane Rebels: Evangelicalism and Antislavery in Antebellum America* (Metuchen, NJ: Scarecrow Press, 1980), 42–51, 71, 78–84.

34. Lawrence, *The Lane Rebels*, 88–89.

35. Ibid., 91–93, 116–118, 126.

36. Ibid., 129–132.

37. Robert S. Fletcher, *A History of Oberlin College: From Its Foundation Through the Civil War*, 2 vols. (Oberlin, OH: Oberlin College, 1943), 1:150–178, 183–184.

38. Recollections of Ezra H. Ferris, quoted in Francis W. Shepardson, *Denison University, 1831–1931: A Centennial History* (Granville, OH: Denison University, 1931), 53.

39. Ferris, quoted in Shepardson, *Denison University*, 53–54.

40. Hamaline McKinney, "History of Muskingum College," 1876?, Box 5, Muskingum College Archives. Herdman's letter against Professor Willson was copied into the August 8, 1856, Trustee Minutes. See Typescript of Trustee Minutes, August 8, 1856, Muskingum College Archives. See also the minutes for August 11 and 28, and September 3, 1856. The September 3 minutes include the notice that the trustees "have

given due attention to the petitions of the citizens of this village" concerning the matter. See also William L. Fisk, "The Early Years of Muskingum College," *The Old Northwest* 5 (1979): 35–38.

41. Daniel Curry et al., "To the Trustees of Indiana Asbury University," November 11, 1856 (broadside), Lilly Library, Indiana University, Bloomington. The letter also appears in the *Putnam Republican Banner* (Greencastle, Indiana), November 19, 1856.

42. Daniel Curry et al., "To the Trustees"; H. W. Cloud et al., "The Students to the Trustees of Indiana Asbury University" (broadside), Lilly Library, Indiana University, Bloomington. The letter appears also in the *Putnam Republican Banner*, November 26, 1856.

43. Daniel Curry et al., "To the Trustees"; H. W. Cloud et al., "The Students to the Trustees" (emphasis original).

44. William Warren Sweet, *Indiana Asbury-DePauw University, 1837–1937: A Hundred Years of Higher Education in the Middle West* (New York: The Abingdon Press, 1937), 71–74.

45. Curry et al., "To the Trustees."

46. Ibid.; H. W. Cloud et al., "The Students to the Trustees"; "The Difficulties in the University," *Putnam Republican Banner*, November 5, 1856.

47. "The Difficulties in the University," *Putnam Republican Banner*, November 5, 1856; "Indiana Asbury University," *Putnam Republican Banner*, November 12, 1856.

48. Joint Board of Trustees and Visitors of the Indiana Asbury University, Minutes, December 16, 1856, Archives, DePauw University, Greencastle, Indiana; Sweet, *Indiana Asbury*, 80–82.

5 / From West to Midwest

1. Donald Worster, *A River Running West: The Life of John Wesley Powell* (New York: Oxford University Press, 2001), 3–27.

2. Ibid., 27–30.

3. Ibid., 30–36.

4. Ibid., 37–70.

5. Ibid., 72, 76–78.

6. Ibid., 72–73, 78–79.

7. Ibid., 73–76.

8. Ibid., 79–82.

9. Ibid., 85–573.

10. Harvey W. Wiley, *Harvey W. Wiley: An Autobiography* (Indianapolis: Bobbs-Merrill, 1930), 13–27, 38, 46. Wiley's recollections of his early life are substantiated by William Lloyd Fox, "Harvey W. Wiley: The Formative Years" (Ph.D. diss., George Washington University, 1960).

11. Wiley, *Autobiography*, 27, 30–32, 38–40.

12. Ibid., 41.

13. Ibid., 14, 35–44, 59–64.

14. Ibid., 64–66.

15. Ibid., 78–79, 91.

16. Ibid., 55–59, 67–75.

17. Ibid., 81.

18. Ibid., 88–159.

19. Oscar E. Anderson, Jr., *The Health of a Nation: Harvey W. Wiley and the Fight for Pure Food* (Chicago: University of Chicago Press, 1958).

20. Robert M. Crunden, *Ministers of Reform: The Progressives' Achievement in American Civilization, 1889–1920* (1982; Urbana: University of Illinois Press, 1984), ix, 14–15. Crunden was not the first to note the importance of Lincoln in the mind of the Midwest. See Ray Ginger, *Altgeld's America: The Lincoln Ideal Versus Changing Realities* (1958; New York: New Viewpoints, 1973).

21. Crunden, *Ministers of Reform*, 277, 64, 7.

22. Jon C. Teaford, *Cities of the Heartland: The Rise and Fall of the Industrial Midwest* (Bloomington: Indiana University Press, 1993), ix.

23. Ronald Weber, *The Midwestern Ascendancy in American Writing* (Bloomington: Indiana University Press, 1992); Teaford, *Cities of the Heartland*, 155–165.

24. David S. Brown, *Beyond the Frontier: The Midwestern Voice in American Historical Writing* (Chicago: University of Chicago Press, 2009).

25. On patents, see Kathryn Kish Sklar, "Ohio 1903: Heartland of Progressive Reform," in Geoffrey Parker, Richard Sisson, and William Russell Coil, eds. *Ohio and the World, 1753–2053: Essays Toward a New History of Ohio* (Columbus: Ohio State University Press, 2005), 99.

26. Raymond Boryczka and Lorin Lee Cary, *No Strength without Union: An Illustrated History of Ohio Workers, 1803–1980* (Columbus: Ohio Historical Society, 1982), 155; Samuel Crowther, *John H. Patterson: Pioneer in Industrial Welfare* (Garden City, NY: Doubleday, Page, 1923).

27. Daryl Melvin Elliott, "Bishop Milton Wright and the Quest for a Christian America" (Ph.D. diss., Drew University, 1992), 21–26.

28. Ibid., 26–30.

29. Ibid., 32–33.

30. Ibid. Also, on Hartsville University, see O. W. Pentzer, *Hartsville College: Hartsville, Indiana, 1850–1897* (Columbus, IN: O. W. Pentzer & Son, 1928).

31. Elliott, "Bishop Milton Wright," 343–347.

32. James R. Shortridge, *The Middle West: Its Meaning in American Culture* (Lawrence: University Press of Kansas, 1989), 16–20. Shortridge believes that the term "Middle West" was in use prior to 1898 to apply to Kansas and Nebraska, but did not find any examples of such usage. The only exception was that he found "middle western" used by Timothy Flint, in 1827, to describe mostly the area covered by Tennessee.

33. R. H. Knapp and H. B. Goodrich, *Origins of American Scientists* (1952; reprint, New York: Russell & Russell, 1967), passim., 260 (quotation). Knapp and Goodrich used the third (1921) and seventh (1944) editions of *American Men of Science*, with other corroborating sources, to gather 18,000 names of Americans with Ph.D.'s in chemistry, biology, physics, geology, mathematics, astronomy, and psychology. They then matched these people with their undergraduate institutions, and used the number of men graduating from these institutions during the period from 1880 to 1940 to determine what colleges and universities had the highest proportions of their male graduates go on to obtain Ph.D.'s in science. Knapp and Goodrich also did a study of the 50 public universities most productive of scientists and found the same regional pattern.

The top fifty schools, organized by state, beginning in the Midwest, were: Oberlin, Antioch, Marietta, Bluffton, Wooster, Hiram, Miami, and Muskingum (Ohio);

Kalamazoo and Hope (Michigan); Earlham, DePauw, Wabash, and Butler (Indiana); Beloit, Lawrence, and the University of Wisconsin (Wisconsin); the University of Chicago and Eureka (Illinois); Carleton and St. Olaf (Minnesota); Iowa Wesleyan, Cornell, Simpson, and Grinnell (Iowa); Central Methodist, Westminster, and Drury (Missouri); Emporia and Southwestern (Kansas); Nebraska Wesleyan; South Dakota School of Mines; Colorado; Montana State; Utah State and Brigham Young (Utah); Reed and Willamette (Oregon); California Institute of Technology and Pomona (California); Charleston (South Carolina); West Virginia Wesleyan; Johns Hopkins (Maryland); Haverford, Swarthmore, and Lebanon Valley (Pennsylvania); University of Rochester (New York); Wesleyan (Connecticut); Clark and the University of Massachusetts (Massachusetts).

34. Steven Shapin, *The Scientific Life: A Moral History of a Late Modern Vocation* (Chicago: University of Chicago Press, 2008), 45 (emphasis original); Knapp and Goodrich, *Origins of American Scientists*, passim.

35. Knapp and Goodrich, *Origins of American Scientists*, passim.

36. Roger L. Geiger, "The Rise and Fall of Useful Knowledge: Higher Education for Science, Agriculture, and the Mechanic Arts, 1850–1875," in Roger Geiger, ed. *The American College in the Nineteenth Century* (Nashville, TN: Vanderbilt University Press, 2000), 153–168, esp. 155–157; see also Russell H. Chittenden, *History of the Sheffield Scientific School of Yale University, 1846–1922*, 2 vols. (New Haven, CT: Yale University Press, 1928).

37. On the democratic nature of scientific investigation, see Walter H. Conser, Jr., *God and the Natural World: Religion and Science in Antebellum America* (Columbia: University of South Carolina Press, 1993), 10–18; on science as a female discipline, see Kim Tolley, *The Science Education of American Girls: A Historical Perspective* (New York: RoutledgeFalmer, 2003), esp. chapter 2, "Science for Ladies, Classics for Gentlemen."

38. Earle D. Ross, "The Manual Labor Experiment in the Land Grant College," *Mississippi Valley Historical Review* 21 (March 1935): 513–528. On the connections between Progressivism and science, see, for example, the ideas of John C. Burnham, in John D. Buenker, John C. Burnham, and Robert M. Crunden, *Progressivism* (1977; Rochester, VT: Schenkman Books, 1986), 19.

39. Ed Millis, *Jack St. Clair Kilby: A Man of Few Words* (Dallas: Ed Millis Books, 2008), 1–22, (quotations, 5, 66).

40. Lillian Hoddeson and Vicki Daitch, *True Genius: The Life and Science of John Bardeen* (Washington, DC: Joseph Henry Press, 2002), 8–27, (quotation, 14).

41. John Bardeen, "Walter Houser Brattain: February 19, 1902–October 13, 1987," 69–72, in National Academy of Sciences, *Biographical Memoirs* (Washington, DC: National Academy Press, 1994), 63: 69–87; Joel N. Shurkin, *Broken Genius: The Rise and Fall of William Shockley, Creator of the Electronic Age* (London: Macmillan, 2006), 3–21; Leslie Berlin, *The Man Behind the Microchip: Robert Noyce and the Invention of Silicon Valley* (New York: Oxford University Press, 2005), 9, 14.

Differences existed between the Midwest and the West, of course, yet higher education in the Western United States most closely resembled Midwestern higher education, both by adopting coeducation faster than the South or the East, and in the Western production of scientists. On coeducation in the American West, see Andrea G. Radke-Moss, *Bright Epoch: Women and Coeducation in the American West* (Lincoln:

University of Nebraska Press, 2008). On the differences between the regions, see James M. Madison, "Diverging Trails: Why the Midwest is Not the West," in Martin Ridge, Robert C. Ritchie, and Paul Andrew Hutton, eds. *Frontier and Region: Essays in Honor of Martin Ridge* (Albuquerque: University of New Mexico Press, 1997), 43–53.

42. James A. Hijiya, *Lee De Forest and the Fatherhood of Radio* (Bethlehem, PA: Lehigh University Press, 1992).

43. Wolfe, "Two Young Men Who Went West," 58–59.

44. Arthur E. Bestor, Jr., "Patent-Office Models of the Good Society: Some Relationships Between Social Reform and Westward Expansion," in Harry N. Scheiber, ed. *The Old Northwest: Studies in Regional History, 1787–1910* (Lincoln: University of Nebraska Press, 1969), 68–92, (quotation, 89). Bestor found that almost half (45 of 99) of the communitarian societies established between 1805 and 1855 in the United States appeared in the five states of the Old Northwest.

45. James Freeman Clarke to Margaret Fuller, December 19, 1833, quoted in John W. Thomas, *James Freeman Clarke: Apostle of German Culture to America* (Boston: John W. Luce, 1949), 58. On Clarke as a proponent of coeducation, see Mary Leo Joseph Devine, "A Study of the Historical Development of Coeducation in American Higher Education" (Ph.D. diss., Boston College, 1966), 100–101. See also Frank R. Shivers, Jr., "A Western Chapter in the History of American Transcendentalism," *Bulletin of the Historical and Philosophical Society of Ohio* 15 (1957): 117–130; Albert Barnes, "Plea in Behalf of Western Colleges," 11–12, in *Permanent Documents of the Society for the Promotion of Collegiate and Theological Education at the West,* vol. 1 (New York: John F. Trow, 1844–1851). For a more extensive explication of Barnes's ideas, see Jon Gjerde, *The Minds of the West: Ethnocultural Evolution in the Rural Middle West, 1830–1917* (Chapel Hill: University of North Carolina Press, 1997), 1–4.

46. "Discourse on the History, Character, and Prospects of the West: Delivered to the Union Literary Society of Miami University, Oxford, Ohio, at their Ninth Anniversary, September 23, 1834. By Daniel Drake, M.D." (Cincinnati: Truman and Smith, 1834). Reprinted in Henry D. Shapiro and Zane L. Miller, eds. *Physician to the West: Selected Writings of Daniel Drake on Science and Society* (Lexington: The University Press of Kentucky, 1970), 240–259, (quotations, 242).

47. Drake, "Discourse," 242, 244 (emphasis original); A. Wylie, "An Address Delivered Before the Philomathean Society of the Wabash College, By A. Wylie, D.D., July 10, 1838" (Bloomington, IA: Philomathean Society, n.d.) (emphasis original).

48. Drake, "Discourse," 244.

49. Ibid., 245–246.

Conclusion

1. Andrew R. L. Cayton and Susan E. Gray, eds. *The American Midwest: Essays on Regional History* (Bloomington: Indiana University Press, 2001), 3. Andrew R. L. Cayton is justly regarded as the leading historian of the Midwest. He published similar ideas with Peter Onuf in 1990 in *The Midwest and the Nation: Rethinking the History of an American Region* (Bloomington: Indiana University Press, 1990). See esp. 118, where the authors wrote that "[b]y the 1890s, the midwestern bourgeoisie had lost its initiative and surrendered its momentum. . . . the last decade of the nineteenth century marked the end of the dynamic phase of midwestern culture." Cayton has reiterated this interpretation as late as 2007. See Andrew R. L. Cayton, "General Overview,"

in Richard Sisson, Christian Zacher, and Andrew Cayton, eds. *The American Midwest: An Interpretive Encyclopedia* (Bloomington: Indiana University Press, 2007), esp. xix.

Scholars of a region have increasingly turned to the concept of "many Souths" or "many Wests" as a means of enlarging our conceptions and understandings. See, for example, the chapter "Many Souths" in Peter Kolchin, *A Sphinx on the American Land: The Nineteenth-Century South in Comparative Perspective* (Baton Rouge: Louisiana State University Press, 2003), 39–73; and Michael Steiner and David Wrobel, "Many Wests: Discovering a Dynamic Western Regionalism," in David M. Wrobel and Michael C. Steiner, eds. *Many Wests: Place, Culture, and Regional Identity* (Lawrence: University Press of Kansas, 1997), 1–30. See also Timothy R. Mahoney and Wendy J. Katz, eds. *Regionalism and the Humanities* (Lincoln: University of Nebraska Press, 2008).

2. Sinclair Lewis, *Babbitt* (New York: Harcourt, Brace and Company, 1922), 2, 3.

3. Sinclair Lewis, *Arrowsmith* (New York: Harcourt, Brace and Company, 1925 [1924]). As it happens, Lewis did not accept the Pulitzer Prize.

4. Sinclair Lewis, *Arrowsmith*, 1.

5. Ibid., 15, 31–32.

6. Ibid., 19, 308.

7. P. J. McInernay and J. L. Anderson, "Prize Winners: Selected Listings of Awards Given at Three Major European Film Festivals and by Five American Motion Picture Organizations," *Journal of the University Film Association* 22 (1970): 83; Steven Shapin, *The Scientific Life: A Moral History of a Late Modern Vocation* (Chicago: University of Chicago Press, 2008), 60–63. On the popularity of *Arrowsmith*, see Mark Schorer, "Afterword," in the Signet Classic edition of *Arrowsmith* (New York: New American Library, 1953; afterword, 1961), 438; Sisson, Zacher, and Cayton, *The American Midwest*.

8. Warren I. Susman, *Culture as History: The Transformation of American Society in the Twentieth Century* (New York: Pantheon Books, 1984), 36; Robert L. Dorman, *Revolt of the Provinces: The Regionalist Movement in America, 1920–1945* (Chapel Hill: University of North Carolina Press, 1993), 18.

9. Richard Hofstadter and C. DeWitt Hardy, *The Development and Scope of Higher Education in the United States* (New York: Columbia University Press, 1952), 19; Richard Hofstadter, "The Revolution in Higher Education," in Arthur M. Schlesinger, Jr., and Morton White, eds. *Paths of American Thought* (Boston: Houghton Mifflin Company, 1963), 269–271; Hofstadter and Hardy, *Development and Scope*, 13–14, 17, 20–22; Richard Hofstadter and Walter P. Metzger, *The Development of Academic Freedom in the United States* (New York: Columbia University Press, 1955), 214–215.

10. Hofstadter and Metzger, *The Development of Academic Freedom*, 214–215, 209, 223; Hofstadter and Hardy, *Development and Scope*, 17; Richard Hofstadter and Wilson Smith, eds. *American Higher Education: A Documentary History*, 2 vols. (Chicago: University of Chicago Press, 1961), 1:394; Hofstadter and Metzger, *Development of Academic Freedom*, 211, xii.

11. Alan Brinkley, "Richard Hofstadter's *The Age of Reform*: A Reconsideration," *Reviews in American History* 13 (September 1985): 463; Richard Hofstadter, *The Age of Reform: From Bryan to F.D.R.* (New York: Knopf, 1963), 20.

12. Andrew R. L. Cayton, "The Anti-Region: Place and Identity in the History of the American Midwest," in Cayton and Gray, eds., *The American Midwest*, 143.

BIBLIOGRAPHY

Manuscript Collections

Bentley Historical Library, University of Michigan, Ann Arbor

Copley Family Papers
Horace Wellington Letter

Cincinnati Historical Society

Freeman G. Cary, "Early Annals—Autobiography"

Archives, Denison University, Granville, Ohio

Journal of the Calliopean Society of Granville Institution, Vol. 1, 1835
Office Files

Archives, DePauw University, Greencastle, Indiana

Matthew Simpson Papers
Minutes, Joint Board of Trustees and Visitors of the Indiana Asbury University

Burton Historical Collection, Detroit Public Library

Marion Morse Davis Papers

Archives, Hanover College, Hanover, Indiana

John Finley Crowe Papers

Illinois State Historical Society, Springfield, Illinois

"Autobiography of John Calvin Hanna," SC 645
Riggin Family Papers

Indiana Historical Society, Indianapolis

Asbury Wilkinson Papers
Timothy Horton Ball Papers

Indiana State Library, Indianapolis

Church History—American Home Missionary Society Mss., L 187
Diary of Elijah Evan Edwards, L 49
Edmund O. Hovey Papers

Special Collections, Kenyon College, Gambier, Ohio

Chase Papers

Library of Congress, Washington, D.C.

Benjamin Harrison Papers (microfilm edition)
Bishop Matthew Simpson Papers

Lilly Library, Indiana University, Bloomington

Bartholomew mss.
Daniel Curry, et al. "To the Trustees of Indiana Asbury University"
H. W. Cloud, et al. "The Students to the Trustees of Indiana Asbury University"
Stevens mss. II

Archives, Muskingum College, New Concord, Ohio

Hamaline McKinney, "History of Muskingum College"
Trustee Minutes

Archives, Oberlin College, Oberlin, Ohio

John J. Shipherd Papers
Letters Received by Oberlin College, 1822–1866
Oberlin File
Robert S. Fletcher Papers

Ohio Historical Society, Columbus, Ohio

VFM 783
Allen Missionary Lyceum, Constitution and By-Laws, VFM 223
Dana Family Papers
John A. Trimble Family Papers, MSS 249
King Family Papers, MSS 40
Princess A. Miller Autograph Book

Samuel Williams and Samuel Wesley Williams Papers, MSS 148

Ohio Wesleyan Historical Collections, Ohio Wesleyan University, Delaware, Ohio

Early OWU Letters
Morris Papers

Western Reserve Historical Society, Cleveland, Ohio

John Stevens Papers, MSS 1455
Thomas, Wheeler and White Family Papers, MSS 3412

Published Primary Sources

"Catalogue of the East Alabama Masonic Female Institute, of Talladega, Alabama." Montgomery: Advertiser and Gazette Steam Power Press Book Office, 1854.

"The Catalogue of the Officers and Students of Franklin College, New Athens, Ohio; 1848." St. Clairsville, Ohio: William Brown, 1848.

"Catalogue of the Officers & Students of the Michigan Central College, at Spring Arbor, for the year ending January 1852." Detroit: Duncklee, Wales & Co., 1852.

"Catalogue of the Officers and Students of the Ohio Wesleyan University, for the Academical Year 1844-5. Delaware, Ohio." Columbus: S. Medary, 1845.

"Catalogue of the Officers and Students of the Southern Masonic Female College at Covington, Georgia." Atlanta: C. R. Hanleiter & Co., 1856.

"Catalogue of the Zetagathean Society of the Ohio Wesleyan University, Delaware, Ohio, 1845-'52." Columbus: Scott & Bascom, 1852.

Chase, Philander. "The Star in the West, or Kenyon College, in the Year of our Lord, 1828." Columbus: n.p., 1828.

"Discourse on the History, Character, and Prospects of the West: Delivered to the Union Literary Society of Miami University, Oxford, Ohio, at their Ninth Anniversary, September 23, 1834. By Daniel Drake, M.D." Cincinnati: Truman and Smith, 1834. Reprinted in *Physician to the West: Selected Writings of Daniel Drake on Science and Society*, edited by Henry D. Shapiro and Zane L. Miller, 240–259. Lexington: The University Press of Kentucky, 1970.

"The First Report of the Society for the Promotion of Collegiate and Theological Education at the West." New York: J. F. Trow & Co., 1844.

"The Fourth Report of the Society for the Promotion of Collegiate and Theological Education at the West." New York: Leavitt, Trow and Company, 1847.

Mann, Horace. "Demands of the Age on Colleges: Speech Delivered by the Hon. Horace Mann, President of Antioch College, Before the Christian Convention, at its Quadrennial Session, Held at Cincinnati, Ohio, October 5, 1854." New York: Fowler & Wells, 1857.

"'Old Woodward': A Memorial Relating to Woodward High School, 1831–1836, & Woodward College, 1836–1851, in the City of Cincinnati."

Permanent Documents of the Society for the Promotion of Collegiate and Theological Education at the West. New York: John F. Trow, 1844–1851.

"Second Report of the Society for the Promotion of Collegiate and Theological Education at the West." New York: J. F. Trow & Co., 1845.

Smith, Delazon. *A History of Oberlin, Or New Lights of the West.* Cleveland: S. Underhill & Son, 1837.

Storrs, Charles B. "An Address, Delivered at the Western Reserve College, Hudson, Ohio, February 9, 1831." Boston: Peirce and Parker, 1831.

Thomson, Edward. "Inaugural Address, Delivered at the Ohio Wesleyan University, Delaware, Ohio, at its Annual Commencement, Aug. 6, 1846." Cincinnati: R. P. Thompson, 1846.

Weld, Theodore D. *First Annual Report of the Society for Promoting Manual Labor in Literary Institutions.* New York: S. W. Benedict, 1833.

"Western Colleges; a Baccalaureate Address, Delivered July 22, 1847, by Rev. Charles White, D.D., President of Wabash College." New York: C. W. Benedict, 1848.

Wylie, A. "An Address Delivered Before the Philomathean Society of the Wabash College, By A. Wylie, D.D., July 10, 1838." Bloomington, Indiana: Philomathean Society, n.d.

Newspapers and Periodicals

The Advance (Hillsdale, Michigan), 1886
The Charleston Gospel Messenger, and Protestant Episcopal Register (1839)
Cincinnatus (Cincinnati, Ohio), 1856–1858
North American Review (Boston), 1883
The Oberlin News (Oberlin, Ohio), 1904
Putnam Republican Banner (Greencastle, Indiana), 1856
The Reunion (Hillsdale, Michigan), 1885
Wesleyan Christian Advocate (Cincinnati, Ohio), 1842

Articles and Book Chapters

Allardice, Bruce. "West Points of the Confederacy: Southern Military Schools and the Confederate Army." *Civil War History* 43 (1997): 310–331.

Axtell, James. "The Death of the Liberal Arts College." *History of Education Quarterly* 11 (1971): 339–352.

Bardeen, John. "Walter Houser Brattain: February 19, 1902–October 13, 1987." In National Academy of Sciences, *Biographical Memoirs*, 69–72. Washington, DC: National Academy Press, 1994.

Becker, Carl M. "Freeman Cary and Farmers' College: An Ohio Educator and an Experiment in Nineteenth Century 'Practical' Education." *Bulletin of the Historical and Philosophical Society of Ohio* 21 (July 1963): 150–178.

Becker, Carl M. "The Patriarch of Farmers' College," *Bulletin of the Cincinnati Historical Society* 23 (1965): 104–118.

Bestor, Arthur E., Jr. "Patent-Office Models of the Good Society: Some Relationships Between Social Reform and Westward Expansion." In *The Old Northwest: Studies in Regional History, 1787–1910*, edited by Harry N. Scheiber, 68–92. Lincoln: University of Nebraska Press, 1969.

Boase, Paul H. "Interdenominational Polemics on the Ohio Frontier." *Bulletin of the Historical and Philosophical Society of Ohio* 20 (April 1962): 98–110.

Breunig, Charles. "The Founding of Lawrence University: Aims of Absentee Philanthropist Revised to Fit Fox River Region." *Voyageur: Historical Review of Brown County and Northeast Wisconsin* 9 (1993): 2–14.

Brinkley, Alan. "Richard Hofstadter's *The Age of Reform*: A Reconsideration." *Reviews in American History* 13 (September 1985): 462–480.

Cammack, Eleanore, ed. "Cyrus Nutt Becomes a Hoosier." *Indiana Magazine of History* 53 (1957): 52–65.

Cayton, Andrew R. L. "The Anti-Region: Place and Identity in the History of the American Midwest." In *The American Midwest: Essays on Regional History*, edited by Andrew R. L. Cayton and Susan E. Gray, 140–159. Bloomington: Indiana University Press, 2001.

Cayton, Andrew R. L. "The Middle West." In *A Companion to 19th-Century America*, edited by William L. Barney, 272–285. Malden, MA: Blackwell Publishing, 2001.

Conway, Jill. "Perspectives on the History of Women's Education in the United States." *History of Education Quarterly* 14 (1974): 1–12.

Davis, James E. "'New Aspects of Men and New Forms of Society': The Old Northwest, 1790–1820." *Journal of the Illinois State Historical Society* 69 (1976): 164–172.

Dunbar, Willis. "Public versus Private Control of Higher Education in Michigan, 1817–1855." *Mississippi Valley Historical Review* 22 (1935): 385–406.

Durrill, Wayne K. "The Power of Ancient Words: Classical Teaching and Social Change at South Carolina College, 1804–1860." *Journal of Southern History* 65 (1999): 469–498.

"Early History of Olivet College." *Michigan Historical Collections* 3 (1879–1880): 408–414.

Elkins, Stanley, and Eric McKitrick. "A Meaning for Turner's Frontier: Part I: Democracy in the Old Northwest." *Political Science Quarterly* 69 (1954): 321–353.

Ellsworth, Clayton S. "Ohio's Legislative Attack upon Abolition Schools," *Mississippi Valley Historical Review* 21 (1934): 379–386.

Findlay, James. "Agency, Denominations and the Western Colleges, 1830–1860: Some Connections between Evangelicalism and American Higher Education." *Church History* 50 (1981): 64–80.

Fisk, William. "The Associate Reformed Church Marches Westward." In *Buckeye Presbyterianism*, edited by E. B. Welsh, 48–61. N.p.: n.p., 1968.

Fisk, William L. "The Early Years of Muskingum College." *The Old Northwest* 5 (1979): 19–44.

Fletcher, Robert S. "Oberlin and Co-Education." *Ohio State Archaeological and Historical Quarterly* 47 (1938): 1–19.

Geiger, Roger L. "Introduction: New Themes in the History of Nineteenth-Century Colleges." In *The American College in the Nineteenth Century*, edited by Roger Geiger, 1–36. Nashville, TN: Vanderbilt University Press, 2000.

Ginzberg, Lori D. "The 'Joint Education of the Sexes': Oberlin's Original Vision." In *Educating Men and Women Together: Coeducation in a Changing World*, edited by Carol Lasser, 67–80. Urbana: University of Illinois Press, 1987.

———. "Women in an Evangelical Community: Oberlin, 1835–1850." *Ohio History* 89 (Winter 1980): 78–88.

Goldstein, Linda Lehmann. "'Without Compromising in Any Particular': The Success of Medical Coeducation in Cleveland, 1850–1856." *Caduceus: A Museum Quarterly for the Health Sciences* 10 (1994): 101–116.

Goodman, Paul. "The Manual Labor Movement and the Origins of Abolitionism." *Journal of the Early Republic* 13 (1993): 355–388.

Graham, Patricia Albjerg. "Expansion and Exclusion: A History of Women in American Higher Education." *Signs: Journal of Women in Culture and Society* 3 (1978): 759–773.

Gruenwald, Kim M. "Space and Place on the Early American Frontier: The Ohio Valley as a Region, 1790–1850." *Ohio Valley History* 4 (Fall 2004): 31–48.

Herbst, Jurgen. "The Development of Public Universities in the Old Northwest." In *The Northwest Ordinance: Essays on Its Formulation, Provisions, and Legacy*, edited by Frederick D. Williams, 97–117. East Lansing: Michigan State University Press, 1989.

"Historical Sketch of the Ohio Wesleyan Female College, Delaware, Ohio," *Historical Sketches of the Higher Educational Institutions, and also of Benevolent and Reformatory Institutions of the State of Ohio* (Columbus, OH: Ohio Commissioner of Common Schools, 1876).

Hofstadter, Richard. "The Revolution in Higher Education." In *Paths of American Thought*, edited by Arthur M. Schlesinger, Jr. and Morton White, 269–290. Boston: Houghton Mifflin Company, 1963.

Hogeland, Ronald W. "Coeducation of the Sexes at Oberlin College: A Study of Social Ideas in Mid-Nineteenth-Century America." *Journal of Social History* 6 (1972–1973): 160–176.

Huth, Ronald K. "Louis Kossuth in Ohio." *Northwest Ohio Quarterly* 40 (1968): 111–117.

Johnson, Daniel T. "Financing the Western Colleges, 1844–1862." *Journal of the Illinois State Historical Society* 65 (1972): 43–54.

Kerns, Kathryn M. "Farmers' Daughters: The Education of Women at Alfred Academy and University Before the Civil War." *History of Higher Education Annual* 6 (1986): 11–28.

Knight, Edgar W. "Manual Labor Schools in the South." *South Atlantic Quarterly* 16 (1917): 209–221.

Madison, James M. "Diverging Trails: Why the Midwest is Not the West." In *Frontier and Region: Essays in Honor of Martin Ridge*, edited by Martin Ridge, Robert C. Ritchie, and Paul Andrew Hutton, 43–53. Albuquerque: University of New Mexico Press, 1997.

Malkmus, Doris. "Origins of Coeducation in Antebellum Iowa." *The Annals of Iowa* 58 (Spring 1999): 162–196.

McCandless, Amy Thompson. "Maintaining the Spirit and Tone of Robust Manliness: The Battle against Coeducation at Southern Colleges and Universities, 1890–1940." *NWSA Journal* 2 (1990): 199–216.

McInernay, P. J. and J. L. Anderson, "Prize Winners: Selected Listings of Awards Given at Three Major European Film Festivals and by Five American Motion Picture Organizations," *Journal of the University Film Association* 22 (1970): 59–94.

McLachlan, James. "The American College in the Nineteenth Century: Toward a Reappraisal." *Teachers College Record* 80 (1978): 287–306.

———. "The *Choice of Hercules*: American Student Societies in the Early 19th Century." In *The University in Society: Europe, Scotland, and the United States from the 16th to the 20th Century*, edited by Lawrence Stone, 2:449–494. 2 vols. Princeton, NJ: Princeton University Press, 1974.

"Memorabilia of an Earlier Student." *DePauw Alumnus* (November 1958.)

Miller, Edward A. "The History of Educational Legislation in Ohio from 1803 to 1850." *Ohio Archaeological and Historical Quarterly* 27 (January–April 1918): 1–271.

Naylor, Natalie. "The Antebellum College Movement: A Reappraisal of Tewksbury's Founding of American Colleges and Universities." *History of Education Quarterly* 13 (1973): 261–274.

Persons, Stow. "The Cyclical Theory of History in Eighteenth Century America." *American Quarterly* 6 (1954): 147–163.

Potts, David B. "American Colleges in the Nineteenth Century: From Localism to Denominationalism." *History of Education Quarterly* 11 (1971): 363–380.

Ringenberg, William C. "The Oberlin College Influence in Early Michigan." *The Old Northwest* 3 (1977): 111–131.

Rosenberg, Rosalind. "The Limits of Access: The History of Coeducation in America." In *Women and Higher Education in American History: Essays From the Mount Holyoke College Sesquicentennial Symposia*, edited by John Mack Faragher and Florence Howe, 107–129. New York: W. W. Norton & Company, 1988.

Ross, Earle D. "The Manual Labor Experiment in the Land Grant College." *Mississippi Valley Historical Review* 21 (1935): 513–528.

Rotundo, E. Anthony. "Body and Soul: Changing Ideals of American Middle-Class Manhood, 1770–1920." *Journal of Social History* 16 (1983): 23–38.

Rury, John, and Glenn Harper. "The Trouble with Coeducation: Mann and

Women at Antioch, 1853–1860." *History of Education Quarterly* 26 (1986): 481–502.

Shivers, Frank R., Jr. "A Western Chapter in the History of American Transcendentalism." *Bulletin of the Historical and Philosophical Society of Ohio* 15 (1957): 117–130.

Sklar, Kathryn Kish. "Ohio 1903: Heartland of Progressive Reform." In *Ohio and the World, 1753–2053: Essays Toward a New History of Ohio*, edited by Geoffrey Parker, Richard Sisson, and William Russell Coil, 95–127. Columbus: Ohio State University Press, 2005.

Smith, Ophia D. "The New Jerusalem Church in Ohio From 1848 to 1870." *Ohio State Archaeological and Historical Quarterly* 62 (January 1953): 25–54.

Smith, Timothy L. "The Ohio Valley: Testing Ground for America's Experiment in Religious Pluralism." *Church History* 60 (1991): 461–479.

———. "Uncommon Schools: Christian Colleges and Social Idealism in Midwestern America, 1820–1950." In *Indiana Historical Society Lectures, 1976–1977: The History of Education in the Middle West*. Indianapolis: Indiana Historical Society, 1978.

Smith, William E., and Ophia D. Smith, eds. "The Diary of Charles Peabody." *Bulletin of the Historical and Philosophical Society of Ohio* 11 (1953): 274–292.

Smith, Wilson. "Apologia pro Alma Matre: The College as Community in Ante-Bellum America." In *The Hofstadter Aegis: A Memorial*, edited by Stanley Elkins and Eric McKitrick, 125–153. New York: Alfred A. Knopf, 1974.

Solomon, Barbara Miller. "The Oberlin Model and Its Impact on Other Colleges." In *Educating Men and Women Together: Coeducation in a Changing World*, edited by Carol Lasser, 81–90. Urbana: University of Illinois Press, 1987.

Steiner, Michael, and David Wrobel. "Many Wests: Discovering a Dynamic Western Regionalism." In *Many Wests: Place, Culture, and Regional Identity*, edited by David M. Wrobel and Michael C. Steiner, 1–30. Lawrence: University Press of Kansas, 1997.

Stevens, W. Le Conte. "University Education for Women." *North American Review* 136 (1883): 30.

Taylor, Richard S. "Western Colleges as 'Securities of Intelligence & Virtue': The Towne-Eddy Report of 1846." *The Old Northwest* 7 (1981): 41–66.

Urofsky, Melvin I. "Reforms and Response: The Yale Report of 1828." *History of Education Quarterly* 5 (1965): 53–67.

Waite, Frederick C. "Manual Labor, an Experiment in American Colleges of the Early Nineteenth Century." *Association of American Colleges Bulletin* 36 (1950): 391–400.

Weisenburger, Francis P. "The Urbanization of the Middle West: Town and Village in the Pioneer Period." *Indiana Magazine of History* 41 (1945): 19–30.

West, Earl Irvin. "Early Cincinnati's 'Unprecedented Spectacle.'" *Ohio History* 79 (Winter 1970): 5–17.

Wheeler, Kenneth H. "Higher Education in the Antebellum Ohio Valley: Slavery, Sectionalism, and the Erosion of Regional Identity." *Ohio Valley History* 8 (Spring 2008): 1–22.

———. "How Colleges Shaped a Public Culture of Usefulness." In *The Center of a Great Empire: The Ohio Country in the Early American Republic*, edited by Andrew R. L. Cayton and Stuart D. Hobbs, 105–121. Athens: Ohio University Press, 2005.

Williams, S. W. "The Ohio Wesleyan University." *National Repository* 1 (June 1877): 486–487.

Willis, Gwendolyn B., ed. and compiler. "Olympia Brown, An Autobiography." *Annual Journal of the Universalist Historical Society* 4 (1963): 1–12.

Wilson, Carl B. "The Baptist Manual Labor School Movement in the United States." *The Baylor Bulletin* 40 (December 1937): 1–159.

Wolfe, Tom. "Two Young Men Who Went West." In *Hooking Up*. New York: Farrar, Straus, and Giroux, 2000.

Books

Abzug, Robert H. *Passionate Liberator: Theodore Dwight Weld and the Dilemma of Reform*. New York: Oxford University Press, 1980.

Alley, Reuben E. *History of the University of Richmond, 1830–1971*. Charlottesville: University Press of Virginia, 1977.

Allmendinger, David F., Jr. *Paupers and Scholars: The Transformation of Student Life in Nineteenth-Century New England*. New York: St. Martin's Press, 1975.

Anderson, Benedict R. O'G. *Imagined Communities: Reflections on the Origin and Spread of Nationalism*. London: Verso, 1983.

Anderson, Oscar E., Jr. *The Health of a Nation: Harvey W. Wiley and the Fight for Pure Food*. Chicago: University of Chicago Press, 1958.

Andrew, Rod, Jr. *Long Gray Lines: The Southern Military School Tradition, 1839–1915*. Chapel Hill: University of North Carolina Press, 2001.

Aron, Stephen. *How the West Was Lost: The Transformation of Kentucky from Daniel Boone to Henry Clay*. Baltimore: The Johns Hopkins University Press, 1996.

Baxter, Norman Allen. *History of the Freewill Baptists: A Study in New England Separatism*. Rochester, NY: American Baptist Historical Society, 1957.

Beadie, Nancy, and Kim Tolley, eds. *Chartered Schools: Two Hundred Years of Independent Academies in the United States, 1727–1925*. New York: RoutledgeFalmer, 2002.

Beaty, Mary D. *A History of Davidson College*. Davidson, NC: Briarpatch Press, 1988.

Beauregard, Erving E. *Old Franklin, the Eternal Touch: A History of Franklin College, New Athens, Harrison County, Ohio*. Lanham, MD: University Press of America, 1983.

Behney, J. Bruce, and Paul H. Eller. *The History of the Evangelical United Brethren Church*. Kenneth W. Krueger, ed. Nashville, TN: Abingdon, 1979.

Bennett, Charles Alpheus. *History of Manual and Industrial Education up to 1870*. Peoria, IL: The Manual Arts Press, 1926.

Berlin, Leslie. *The Man Behind the Microchip: Robert Noyce and the Invention of Silicon Valley*. New York: Oxford University Press, 2005.

Bond, Beverley W., Jr. *The Civilization of the Old Northwest: A Study of Political, Social, and Economic Development, 1788–1812*. New York: The Macmillan Company, 1934.

Bone, Winstead Paine. *A History of Cumberland University, 1842–1935*. Lebanon, TN: The Author, 1935.

Boorstin, Daniel J. *The Americans: The National Experience*. New York: Vintage Books, 1965.

Boryczka, Raymond, and Lorin Lee Cary. *No Strength without Union: An Illustrated History of Ohio Workers, 1803–1980*. Columbus: Ohio Historical Society, 1982.

Brekus, Catherine A. *Strangers and Pilgrims: Female Preaching in America, 1740–1845*. Chapel Hill: University of North Carolina Press, 1998.

Brown, David S. *Beyond the Frontier: The Midwestern Voice in American Historical Writing*. Chicago: University of Chicago Press, 2009.

Brown, Olympia. *Acquaintances, Old and New, Among Reformers*. Milwaukee: S. E. Tate, 1911.

Brubacher, John S., and Willis Rudy. *Higher Education in Transition: A History of American Colleges and Universities, 1636–1968*. 1958. Revised and enlarged ed. New York: Harper & Row, 1968.

Bruce, Philip Alexander. *History of the University of Virginia, 1819–1919*. 5 vols. New York: The Macmillan Company, 1920.

Buenker, John D., John C. Burnham, and Robert M. Crunden. *Progressivism*. 1977. Rochester, VT: Schenkman Books, 1986.

Buley, R. Carlyle. *The Old Northwest: Pioneer Period, 1815–1840*. 2 vols. Bloomington: Indiana University Press, 1950.

Bullock, Henry Morton. *A History of Emory University*. Nashville, TN: Parthenon Press, 1936.

Burke, Colin B. *American Collegiate Populations: A Test of the Traditional View*. New York: New York University Press, 1982.

Cabaniss, James Allen. *A History of the University of Mississippi*. University, MS: University of Mississippi, 1949.

Cash, W. J. *The Mind of the South*. New York: Vintage Books, 1941.

Caswall, Henry. *America and the American Church*. 1839. New York: Arno Press and the New York Times, 1969.

Cayton, Andrew R. L., and Susan Gray, eds. *The American Midwest: Essays on Regional History*. Bloomington: Indiana University Press, 2001.

Cayton, Andrew R. L., and Peter S. Onuf. *The Midwest and the Nation: Rethink-*

ing the History of an American Region. Bloomington: Indiana University Press, 1990.

Chittenden, Russell H. *History of the Sheffield Scientific School of Yale University, 1846–1922.* 2 vols. New Haven, CT: Yale University Press, 1928.

Clark, Willis G. *History of Education in Alabama, 1702–1889.* Washington, DC: Government Printing Office, 1889.

Conser, Walter H., Jr. *God and the Natural World: Religion and Science in Antebellum America.* Columbia: University of South Carolina Press, 1993.

Cott, Nancy F. *The Bonds of Womanhood: "Woman's Sphere" in New England, 1780–1835.* New Haven: Yale University Press, 1977.

Coulter, E. Merton. *College Life in the Old South.* Athens: University of Georgia Press, 1928.

Cremin, Lawrence A. *American Education: The National Experience, 1783–1876.* New York: Harper and Row, 1980.

Crenshaw, Ollinger. *General Lee's College: The Rise and Growth of Washington and Lee University.* New York: Random House, 1969.

Crook, Isaac. *The Great Five: The First Faculty of the Ohio Wesleyan University.* Cincinnati, OH: Jennings and Graham; New York: Eaton and Mains, 1908.

Crowther, Samuel. *John H. Patterson: Pioneer in Industrial Welfare.* Garden City, NY: Doubleday, Page, 1923.

Crunden, Robert M. *Ministers of Reform: The Progressives' Achievement in American Civilization, 1889–1920.* 1982. Urbana: University of Illinois Press, 1984.

Curran, Robert Emmett. *The Bicentennial History of Georgetown University: From Academy to University, 1789–1889.* Washington, DC: Georgetown University Press, 1993.

Daley, John M. *Georgetown University: Origin and Early Years.* Washington, DC: Georgetown University Press, 1957.

Daniel, Robert Norman. *Furman University: A History.* Greenville, SC: Furman University, 1951.

Davenport, F. Garvin. *Monmouth College: The First Hundred Years, 1853–1953.* Cedar Rapids, IA: The Torch Press, 1953.

Dexter, Elisabeth Anthony. *Career Women of America, 1776–1840.* Francestown, NH: Marshall Jones Company, 1950.

Dorman, Robert L. *Revolt of the Provinces: The Regionalist Movement in America, 1920–1945.* Chapel Hill: University of North Carolina Press, 1993.

Dowell, Spright. *A History of Mercer University, 1833–1953.* Macon, GA: Mercer University, 1958.

Dunbar, Willis F. *The Michigan Record in Higher Education.* Detroit: Wayne State University Press, 1963.

Durkin, Joseph, ed. *Swift Potomac's Lovely Daughter: Two Centuries at Georgetown through Students' Eyes.* Washington, DC: Georgetown University Press, 1990.

Durkin, Joseph T. *Georgetown University: The Middle Years (1840–1900)*. Washington, DC: Georgetown University Press, 1963.

Easterby, J. H. *A History of the College of Charleston, Founded 1770*. N.p.: Scribner Press, 1935.

Eaton, Clement. *Freedom of Thought in the Old South*. Durham, NC: Duke University Press, 1940.

Ekirch, Arthur A., Jr. *The Idea of Progress in America, 1815–1860*. New York: Peter Smith, 1944; reprint, New York: Columbia University Press, 1951.

Ellis, William Arba, ed. *Norwich University, 1819–1911: Her History, Her Graduates, Her Roll of Honor*. 3 vols. Montpelier, VT: Capital City Press, 1911.

England, J. Merton, ed. *Buckeye Schoolmaster: A Chronicle of Midwestern Rural Life, 1853–1865*. Bowling Green, OH: Bowling Green State University Popular Press, 1996.

Fairchild, J. H. *Oberlin. Its Origin, Progress and Results*. Oberlin, OH: R. Butler, 1871.

Farnham, Christie Anne. *The Education of the Southern Belle: Higher Education and Student Socialization in the Antebellum South*. New York: New York University Press, 1995.

Fletcher, Robert S. *A History of Oberlin College: From Its Foundation Through the Civil War*. 2 vols. Oberlin, OH: Oberlin College, 1943.

Gamble, Paul. *History of Westminster College, 1852–1977*. New Wilmington, PA: Westminster College, 1977.

Garst, Henry. *Otterbein University, 1847–1907*. Dayton, OH: United Brethren Publishing House, 1907.

Gates, Helen Dunn. *A Consecrated Life: A Sketch of the Life and Labors of Rev. Ransom Dunn, D.D. 1818–1900*. Boston: Morning Star Publishing House, 1901.

Geiger, Roger, ed. *The American College in the Nineteenth Century*. Nashville, TN: Vanderbilt University Press, 2000.

Ginger, Ray. *Altgeld's America: The Lincoln Ideal Versus Changing Realities*. 1958. New York: New Viewpoints, 1973.

Gjerde, Jon. *The Minds of the West: Ethnocultural Evolution in the Rural Middle West, 1830–1917*. Chapel Hill: University of North Carolina Press, 1997.

Godbold, Albea. *The Church College of the Old South*. Durham, NC: Duke University Press, 1944.

Godson, Susan H., Ludwell H. Johnson, Richard B. Sherman, Thad W. Tate, and Helen C. Walker. *The College of William and Mary: A History. Volume I, 1693–1888*. Williamsburg, VA: King and Queen Press, 1993.

Green, Jennifer R. *Military Education and the Emerging Middle Class in the Old South*. New York, NY: Cambridge University Press, 2008.

Gruenwald, Kim M. *River of Enterprise: The Commercial Origins of Regional Identity in the Ohio Valley, 1790–1850*. Bloomington: Indiana University Press, 2002.

Hamilton, Alice. *Exploring the Dangerous Trades: The Autobiography of Alice Hamilton, M.D.* Boston: Little, Brown and Company, 1943.

Hamm, Thomas D. *Earlham College: A History, 1847–1997.* Bloomington: Indiana University Press, 1997.

———. *The Transformation of American Quakerism: Orthodox Friends, 1800–1907.* Bloomington: Indiana University Press, 1988.

Hammond, William Gardiner. *Remembrance of Amherst: An Undergraduate's Diary, 1846–1848.* George F. Whicher, ed. New York: Columbia University Press, 1946.

Harding, Thomas S. *College Literary Societies: Their Contribution to Higher Education in the United States, 1815–1876.* New York: Pageant Press, 1971.

Hatch, Louis C. *The History of Bowdoin College.* Portland, ME: Loring, Short & Harmon, 1927.

Hatch, Nathan O. *The Democratization of American Christianity.* New Haven: Yale University Press, 1989.

Hesseltine, William B. *Pioneer's Mission: The Story of Lyman Copeland Draper.* Madison: The State Historical Society of Wisconsin, 1954.

Higgins, Frank. *"The Will to Survive": Urbana College, 1850–1975.* Urbana, OH: Urbana College, n.d.

Hijiya, James A. *Lee De Forest and the Fatherhood of Radio.* Bethlehem, PA: Lehigh University Press, 1992.

Hinderaker, Eric. *Elusive Empires: Constructing Colonialism in the Ohio Valley, 1673–1800.* Cambridge, NY: Cambridge University Press, 1997.

Historical Sketches of the Higher Educational Institutions, and also of Benevolent and Reformatory Institutions of the State of Ohio. [Columbus, OH: State Commissioner of Common Schools], 1876.

History of Delaware County and Ohio. Chicago: O. L. Baskin & Co., 1880.

Hoddeson, Lillian, and Vicki Daitch. *True Genius: The Life and Science of John Bardeen.* Washington, DC: Joseph Henry Press, 2002.

Hoeveler, J. David. *Creating the American Mind: Intellect and Politics in the Colonial Colleges.* Lanham, MD: Rowman & Littlefield, 2002.

Hofstadter, Richard. *The Age of Reform: From Bryan to F.D.R.* 1955. New York: Knopf, 1963.

Hofstadter, Richard, and C. DeWitt Hardy. *The Development and Scope of Higher Education in the United States.* New York: Columbia University Press, 1952.

Hofstadter, Richard, and Walter P. Metzger. *The Development of Academic Freedom in the United States.* New York: Columbia University Press, 1955.

Hofstadter, Richard, and Wilson Smith, eds. *American Higher Education: A Documentary History.* 2 vols. Chicago: University of Chicago Press, 1961.

Hollis, Daniel Walker. *South Carolina College.* Vol. 1, *University of South Carolina.* Columbia: University of South Carolina Press, 1951.

Horowitz, Helen Lefkowitz. *Campus Life: Undergraduate Cultures From the End of the Eighteenth Century to the Present.* New York: Alfred A. Knopf, 1987.

Howe, Florence. *Myths of Coeducation: Selected Essays, 1964–1983*. Blooming-ton: Indiana University Press, 1984.

Hubbart, Henry Clyde. *Ohio Wesleyan's First Hundred Years*. Delaware, OH: Ohio Wesleyan University, 1943.

Humble, Bill J. *Campbell and Controversy: The Debates of Alexander Campbell*. Joplin, MO: College Press, 1986.

Huston, A. B. *Historical Sketch of Farmers' College*. N.p.: Students' Association of Farmers' College, n.d.

Kelley, Brooks Mather. *Yale: A History*. New Haven: Yale University Press, 1974.

Kelley, Mary. *Learning to Stand and Speak: Women, Education, and Public Life in America's Republic*. Chapel Hill: University of North Carolina Press, 2006.

King, Ray A. *A History of the Associate Reformed Presbyterian Church*. Char-lotte, NC: Board of Christian Education of the Associate Reformed Presby-terian Church, 1966.

Knapp, R. H., and H. B. Goodrich. *Origins of American Scientists*. Chicago: Uni-versity of Chicago Press, 1952; reprint, New York: Russell & Russell, 1967.

Knight, Edgar W., ed. *A Documentary History of Education in the South Before 1860*. 5 vols. Chapel Hill: University of North Carolina Press, 1953.

Kolchin, Peter. *A Sphinx on the American Land: The Nineteenth-Century South in Comparative Perspective*. Baton Rouge: Louisiana State University Press, 2003.

Lang, John Dunmore. *Religion and Education in America*. London: Thomas Ward and Co., 1840.

Lasser, Carol, and Marlene Deahl Merrill, eds. *Friends and Sisters: Letters be-tween Lucy Stone and Antoinette Brown Blackwell, 1846–93*. Urbana: Univer-sity of Illinois Press, 1987.

———, eds. *Soul Mates: The Oberlin Correspondence of Lucy Stone and Antoi-nette Brown, 1846–1850*. Oberlin, OH: Oberlin College, 1983.

Lawrence, Thomas Lesick. *The Lane Rebels: Evangelicalism and Antislavery in Antebellum America*. Metuchen, NJ: Scarecrow Press, 1980.

Lewis, Alvin Fayette. *History of Higher Education in Kentucky*. Washington, DC: Government Printing Office, 1899.

Lewis, Sinclair. *Arrowsmith*. 1924. New York: Harcourt, Brace and Company, 1925.

———. *Babbitt*. New York: Harcourt, Brace and Company, 1922.

Lucas, Christopher J. *American Higher Education: A History*. New York: St. Martin's Press, 1994.

Mahoney, Timothy R., and Wendy J. Katz, eds. *Regionalism and the Humani-ties*. Lincoln: University of Nebraska Press, 2008.

Mathews, Lois Kimball. *The Expansion of New England: The Spread of New England Settlement and Institutions to the Mississippi River, 1620–1865*. 1909. New York: Russell & Russell, 1962.

McGrane, Reginald C. *The University of Cincinnati: A Success Story in Urban Higher Education*. New York: Harper & Row, 1963.

Mead, David. *Yankee Eloquence in the Middle West: The Ohio Lyceum, 1850–1870*. East Lansing: Michigan State College Press, 1951.

Memorial Record of the Counties of Delaware, Union and Morrow. Chicago: Lewis Publishing Company, 1895.

Meriwether, Colyer. *History of Higher Education in South Carolina*. Washington, DC: Government Printing Office, 1889.

Millis, Ed. *Jack St. Clair Kilby: A Man of Few Words*. Dallas: Ed Millis Books, 2008.

Millis, William Alfred. *The History of Hanover College From 1827 to 1927*. Hanover, IN: Hanover College, 1927.

Mode, Peter G. *The Frontier Spirit in American Christianity*. New York: The Macmillan Company, 1923.

Moore, Vivian Lyon. *The First Hundred Years of Hillsdale College*. Ann Arbor, MI: Ann Arbor Press, 1943.

Murray, Lois Smith. *Baylor at Independence*. Waco, TX: Baylor University Press, 1972.

Nash, Margaret A. *Women's Education in the United States, 1780–1840*. New York: Palgrave Macmillan, 2005.

Nelson, E. T. *Fifty Years of the History of the Ohio Wesleyan University, 1844–1894*. Cleveland, OH: Cleveland Printing and Publishing Company, 1895.

Newcomer, Mabel. *A Century of Higher Education for American Women*. New York: Harper & Brothers, 1959.

Nisbet, Robert. *History of the Idea of Progress*. New York: Basic Books, 1980.

Onuf, Peter S. *Statehood and Union: A History of the Northwest Ordinance*. Bloomington: Indiana University Press, 1987.

Osborne, James Insley, and Theodore Gregory Gronert. *Wabash College: The First Hundred Years, 1832–1932*. Crawfordsville, IN: R. E. Banta, 1932.

Pace, Robert F. *Halls of Honor: College Men in the Old South*. Baton Rouge: Louisiana State University Press, 2004.

Parrington, Vernon Louis. *Main Currents in American Thought: The Romantic Revolution in America, 1800–1860*. Vol. 2. New York: Harcourt, Brace & World, 1927.

Paschal, George Washington. *History of Wake Forest College*. Wake Forest, NC: Wake Forest College, 1935.

Pentzer, O. W. *Hartsville College: Hartsville, Indiana, 1850–1897*. Columbus, IN: O. W. Pentzer & Son, 1928.

Quint, Wilder Dwight. *The Story of Dartmouth*. Boston: Little, Brown, and Company, 1914.

Radke-Moss, Andrea G. *Bright Epoch: Women and Coeducation in the American West*. Lincoln: University of Nebraska Press, 2008.

Reid, T. R. *The Chip: How Two Americans Invented the Microchip and Launched a Revolution*. New York: Random House, 1985.

Rosen, Ruth. *The World Split Open: How the Modern Women's Movement Changed America*. New York: Penguin, 2000.

Rudolph, Frederick. *The American College and University: A History*. New York: Knopf, 1962.

———. *Curriculum: A History of the American Undergraduate Course of Study since 1636*. San Francisco: Jossey-Bass Publishers, 1977.

Rusk, Ralph Leslie. *The Literature of the Middle Western Frontier*. 2 vols. New York: Columbia University Press, 1925.

Saxenian, AnnaLee. *Regional Advantage: Culture and Competition in Silicon Valley and Route 128*. Cambridge: Harvard University Press, 1994.

Scanlon, James Edward. *Randolph-Macon College: A Southern History, 1825–1967*. Charlottesville: University Press of Virginia, 1983.

Schmidt, George P. *The Liberal Arts College: A Chapter in American Cultural History*. New Brunswick, NJ: Rutgers University Press, 1957.

Sellers, James B. *History of the University of Alabama: Vol. I, 1818–1902*. University, AL: University of Alabama Press, 1953.

Shapin, Steven. *The Scientific Life: A Moral History of a Late Modern Vocation*. Chicago: University of Chicago Press, 2008.

Sheldon, Henry D. *Student Life and Customs*. New York: D. Appleton and Company, 1901.

Shepardson, Francis W. *Denison University, 1831–1931: A Centennial History*. Granville, OH: Denison University, 1931.

Shortridge, James R. *The Middle West: Its Meaning in American Culture*. Lawrence: University Press of Kansas, 1989.

Shurkin, Joel N. *Broken Genius: The Rise and Fall of William Shockley, Creator of the Electronic Age*. London: Macmillan, 2006.

Simeone, James. *Democracy and Slavery in Frontier Illinois: The Bottomland Republic*. DeKalb: Northern Illinois University Press, 2000.

Sisson, Richard, Christian Zacher, and Andrew Cayton, eds. *The American Midwest: An Interpretive Encyclopedia*. Bloomington: Indiana University Press, 2007.

Smith, Henry Nash. *Virgin Land: The American West as a Symbol and Myth*. Cambridge, MA: Harvard University Press, 1950.

Smythe, George Franklin. *Kenyon College: Its First Century*. New Haven: Yale University Press, 1924.

Solomon, Barbara Miller. *In the Company of Educated Women: A History of Women and Higher Education in America*. New Haven: Yale University Press, 1985.

Stameshkin, David M. *The Town's College: Middlebury College, 1800–1915*. Middlebury, VT: Middlebury College Press, 1985.

Starring, Charles R., and James O. Knauss. *The Michigan Search for Educational Standards*. Lansing: Michigan Historical Commission, 1968.

Stevenson, George J. *Increase in Excellence: A History of Emory and Henry College*. New York: Appleton-Century-Crofts, 1963.

Susman, Warren I. *Culture as History: The Transformation of American Society in the Twentieth Century.* New York: Pantheon Books, 1984.

Sweet, William Warren. *Indiana Asbury-DePauw University, 1837–1937: A Hundred Years of Higher Education in the Middle West.* New York: The Abingdon Press, 1937.

Tankersley, Allen P. *College Life at Old Oglethorpe.* Athens: University of Georgia Press, 1951.

Teaford, Jon C. *Cities of the Heartland: The Rise and Fall of the Industrial Midwest.* Bloomington: Indiana University Press, 1993.

Tewksbury, Donald G. *The Founding of American Colleges and Universities Before the Civil War: With Particular Reference to the Religious Influences Bearing Upon the College Movement.* 1932. [Hamden, CT]: Archon Books, 1965.

Thelin, John R. *A History of American Higher Education.* Baltimore: The Johns Hopkins University Press, 2004.

Thomas, John W. *James Freeman Clarke: Apostle of German Culture to America.* Boston: John W. Luce, 1949.

Thomson, Edward. *Life of Edward Thomson.* Cincinnati: Cranston & Stowe; New York: Phillips & Hunt, 1885.

Thornbrough, Gayle, ed. *The Diary of Calvin Fletcher.* 9 vols. Indianapolis: Indiana Historical Society, 1972–1983.

Thornburg, Opal. *Earlham: The Story of the College, 1847–1962.* Richmond, IN: Earlham College Press, 1963.

Thrower, Norman J. W. *Original Survey and Land Subdivision: A Comparative Study of the Form and Effect of Contrasting Cadastral Surveys.* Chicago: Rand McNally & Co., 1966.

Tolley, Kim. *The Science Education of American Girls: A Historical Perspective.* New York: RoutledgeFalmer, 2003.

Treat, Payson Jackson. *The National Land System, 1785–1820.* New York: E. B. Treat & Company, 1910.

Tyler, Alice Felt. *Freedom's Ferment: Phases of American Social History from the Colonial Period to the Outbreak of the Civil War.* New York: Harper & Brothers, 1944.

Utter, William T. *Granville: The Story of an Ohio Village.* Granville, OH: Granville Historical Society, Denison University, 1956.

Wall, Joseph Frazier. *Grinnell College in the Nineteenth Century: From Salvation to Service.* Ames: Iowa State University Press, 1997.

Wallace, David Duncan. *History of Wofford College, 1854–1949.* Nashville, TN: Vanderbilt University Press, 1951.

Ward, Henry W. *Western-Leander-Clark College, 1856–1911.* Dayton, OH: Otterbein Press, 1911.

Weber, Ronald. *The Midwestern Ascendancy in American Writing.* Bloomington: Indiana University Press, 1992.

Weisenburger, Francis P. *The Passing of the Frontier: 1825–1850.* Columbus: Ohio State Archaeological and Historical Society, 1941.

Wertenbaker, Thomas Jefferson. *Princeton, 1746–1896.* Princeton, NJ: Princeton University Press, 1946.

Wiley, Harvey W. *Harvey W. Wiley: An Autobiography.* Indianapolis: Bobbs-Merrill, 1930.

Williams, Charles Richard, ed. *Diary and Letters of Rutherford Birchard Hayes: Nineteenth President of the United States.* Columbus: Ohio State Archaeological and Historical Society, 1922.

Williams, E. I. F. *Heidelberg: Democratic Christian College, 1850–1950.* Menasha, WI: George Banta Publishing, 1952.

Williams, Samuel W. *Pictures of Early Methodism in Ohio.* Cincinnati: Jennings and Graham; New York: Eaton and Mains, 1909.

Williard, George W. *The History of Heidelberg College...* Cincinnati: Elm Street Printing, 1879.

Wind, James P. *The Bible and the University: The Messianic Vision of William Rainey Harper.* Atlanta: Scholars Press, 1987.

Woody, Thomas. *A History of Women's Education in the United States.* 2 vols. 1929. New York: Octagon Books, 1966.

Worster, Donald. *A River Running West: The Life of John Wesley Powell.* New York: Oxford University Press, 2001.

Wright, John D., Jr. *Transylvania: Tutor to the West.* Lexington: University Press of Kentucky, 1975.

Wyatt-Brown, Bertram. *Southern Honor: Ethics and Behavior in the Old South.* New York: Oxford University Press, 1982.

Zygmont, Jeffrey. *Microchip: An Idea, Its Genesis, and the Revolution It Created.* Cambridge, MA: Perseus, 2003.

Unpublished Papers, Theses, and Dissertations

Baker, Dean Paul. "The Partridge Connection: Alden Partridge and Southern Military Education." Ph.D. diss., University of North Carolina at Chapel Hill, 1986.

Benson, Theodore Lloyd. "Planters and Hoosiers: The Development of Sectional Society in Antebellum Indiana and Mississippi." Ph.D. diss., University of Virginia, 1990.

Bostrom, Harvey Rader. "Contributions to Higher Education by the Society for the Promotion of Collegiate and Theological Education at the West, 1843–1874." Ph.D. diss., New York University, 1960.

Crowe, J. Finley. "History of Hanover College." Unpublished manuscript. Indiana University, Bloomington.

Devine, Mary Leo Joseph. "A Study of the Historical Development of Co-education in American Higher Education." Ph.D. diss., Boston College, 1966.

Elliott, Daryl Melvin. "Bishop Milton Wright and the Quest for a Christian America." Ph.D. diss., Drew University, 1992.

Fox, William Lloyd. "Harvey W. Wiley: The Formative Years." Ph.D. diss., George Washington University, 1960.

Gabrielse, D. Randall. "Diversity in Church-Associated Colleges in Michigan and Ohio, 1825–1867." M.A. thesis, Michigan State University, 1993.

Gay, Dorothy Ann. "The Tangled Skein of Romanticism and Violence in the Old South: The Southern Response to Abolitionism and Feminism, 1830–1861." Ph.D. diss., University of North Carolina, 1975.

Graham, Laura. "From Patriarchy to Paternalism: Disestablished Clergymen and the Manual Labor School Movement in Antebellum America." Ph.D. diss., University of Rochester, 1993.

Hamilton, Hallie J. "The Role of the Weekly Press in the Proliferation of Colleges in Illinois, 1830–1860." Ed.D. diss., Indiana University, 1968.

Hedrick, Travis Keene, Jr. "Julian Monson Sturtevant and the Moral Machinery of Society: The New England Struggle Against Pluralism in the Old Northwest, 1829–1877." Ph.D. diss., Brown University, 1974.

Ishkanian, Judith Mitchell. "Religion and Honor at Chapel Hill: The College Odyssey of William Sydney Mullins, 1840–1842." Ph.D. diss., University of California, Santa Barbara, 1993.

Johnson, Daniel T. "Puritan Power in Illinois Higher Education Prior to 1870." Ph.D. diss., University of Wisconsin, 1974.

Kelton, Allen. "The University of Nashville, 1850–1875." Ph.D. diss., George Peabody College for Teachers, 1969.

Kerns, Kathryn M. "Antebellum Higher Education for Women in Western New York State." Ph.D. diss., University of Pennsylvania, 1993.

Malkmus, Doris. "Small Towns, Small Sects, and Coeducation: The Origins of Midwestern Rural Gender." History of Education Society, Chicago, Illinois, October 30, 1998.

Malkmus, Doris Jeanne. "Capable Women and Refined Ladies: Two Visions of American Women's Higher Education, 1760–1861." Ph.D. diss., University of Iowa, 2001.

Miller, Francis Joseph. "A History of the Athenaeum of Ohio, 1829–1960." Ed.D. diss., University of Cincinnati, 1964.

Peterson, Charles E., Jr. "Theron Baldwin and Higher Education in the Old Northwest." Ph.D. diss., Johns Hopkins University, 1960.

Reed, Ralph Eugene, Jr. "Fortresses of Faith: Design and Experience at Southern Evangelical Colleges, 1830–1900." Ph.D. diss., Emory University, 1991.

Ringenberg, William C. "The Protestant College on the Michigan Frontier." Ph.D. diss., Michigan State University, 1970.

Rovick, Norman. "The Impact of Religious Revivalism Upon Five Selected Ohio Colleges of the Mid-Nineteenth Century." M.A. thesis,, Ohio State University, 1965.

Saslaw, Rita Segel. "Student Societies: Nineteenth Century Establishment." Ph.D. diss., Case Western Reserve University, 1971.

Schreiber, Stephen T. "American College Student Riots and Disorders Between 1815 and the Civil War." Ed.D. diss., Indiana University, 1979.

Schwalm, Vernon Franklin. "The Historical Development of the Denominational Colleges in the Old Northwest to 1870." Ph.D. diss., University of Chicago, 1926.

Strong, Susan Rumsey. "'The Most Natural Way in the World': Coeducation at Nineteenth-Century Alfred University." Ph.D. diss., University of Rochester, 1995.

Weidner, Heidemarie Z. "Coeducation and Jesuit *Ratio Studiorum* in Indiana: Rhetoric and Composition Instruction at 19th-Century Butler and Notre Dame." Ph.D. diss., University of Louisville, 1991.

Wheeler, Kenneth H. "The Antebellum College in the Old Northwest: Higher Education and the Defining of the Midwest." Ph.D. diss., Ohio State University, 1999.

Index